the *Thrifty* cookbook

the *Thrifty* cookbook

DELICIOUS RECIPES TO FEED YOUR FAMILY ON A BUDGET

RYLAND

PETERS

& SMALL

LONDON NEW YORK

Senior Designer Iona Hoyle

Senior Editor Céline Hughes

Picture Research Emily Westlake

Production Controller Maria Petalidou

Art Director Leslie Harrington

Publishing Director Alison Starling

Indexer Hilary Bird

First published in the UK in 2010
by Ryland Peters & Small
20–21 Jockey's Fields
London WC1R 4BW
www.rylandpeters.com

10 9 8 7 6 5 4 3 2 1

Text © Fiona Beckett, Susannah Blake, Tamsin Burnett-Hall,
Maxine Clark, Linda Collister, Ross Dobson, Liz Franklin,
Tonia George, Nicola Graimes, Jennifer Joyce, Caroline
Marson, Annie Nichols, Jane Noraika, Louise Pickford, Rena
Salaman, Jennie Shapter, Fiona Smith, Sonia Stevenson,
Linda Tubby, Sunil Vijayakar, Fran Warde, Laura Washburn,
Lindy Wildsmith, and Ryland Peters & Small 2010

Design and photographs © Ryland Peters & Small 2010

ISBN: 978-1-84597-962-1

Printed and bound in China

A CIP record for this book is available from
the British Library.

Notes:

• All spoon measurements are level, unless
otherwise specified.

• Ovens should be preheated to the specified
temperature. Recipes in this book were tested using
a regular oven. If using a fan-assisted oven, follow
the manufacturer's instructions for adjusting
temperatures.

• All eggs are medium, unless otherwise specified.
Recipes containing raw or partially cooked egg,
or raw fish or shellfish, should not be served to the
very young, very old, anyone with a compromised
immune system or pregnant women.

contents

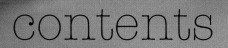

introduction

Being thrifty is often a matter of common sense and a little forward planning. Get into the habit of keeping your storecupboards stocked with useful basic standbys so that you can whip up a nourishing meal even if you haven't been to the supermarket recently – that will remove the temptation to order in a takeaway.

Buy fresh produce when it's in season, which makes it cheaper because it hasn't been flown around the world; and if it's bought from the market, you may be able to get a good deal on a bag of apples or similar at the end of the day.

Instead of reaching for those chicken fillets on your weekly shop, why not buy drumsticks, thighs, or even a whole chicken, which you can joint and make so much from. Pound for pound, it's much more economical. Rediscover the benefits of cooking with cheaper cuts of meat, which often still have the bone(s) in or are less lean – these cuts need more time to cook but the bones and fat are precisely what makes stews, roasts and pies so tasty and mouth-wateringly tender. This is where weekends can be put to such good use, with slow-cooked dishes designed to be enjoyed both on the day and as leftovers during the week.

Leftovers: such an unappealing word for something with so much potential! If you take just one thing from this book, let it be the value of leftovers. Always think about how you can use up the food lurking in your kitchen before going out to buy more. Hopefully this book will help you make the most of surplus mashed potatoes, rice and spaghetti, and that ever-annoying bowl of egg whites left over from your last dessert recipe.

Thrifty cooking needn't be boring. It's about cutting down on waste (thereby helping the environment), making good use of ingredients and finding new, exciting ways to be frugal.

thrifty tips

Sometimes you're missing just one ingredient, or have slightly the wrong flour for your recipe. Sometimes you have a busy week ahead and won't have time to cook. Sometimes a dish goes wrong. Don't panic! Here are some tips to guide you through thrifty cooking.

Every recipe in this book has at least two of these symbols:

 This tells you roughly how many people the recipe should serve

 This is an extra-quick recipe, and shouldn't take you longer than 20 minutes once you've prepared the ingredients.

 This is suitable for vegetarians, but that's not to say that meat-eaters won't enjoy it too!

 This recipe includes some meat or poultry.

 This recipe includes some fish or seafood.

Recipes

• If you have used some eggs for a recipe and are left with unused egg whites, turn to these pages for ways to use them up: 211, 227, 229.

• If you are left with unused egg yolks, turn to these pages: 203, 219, 229, 233, 234.

• Home-made stock can be frozen in handy portions for future use. Pour the cooled stock into the cups of a non-stick muffin tin and freeze until solid. Remove the frozen blocks from the muffin tin, put them in a freezer bag, seal, label and freeze, Remove stock portions as you need them. See also stock recipes on page 53 and 54 for more storage tips.

• Make a double quantity of crumble topping (see recipes on pages 212–217) and freeze half for next time. Break into small pieces and sprinkle it over the fruit before baking – there is no need to defrost it first.

Ingredients

• If a recipe calls for snipped fresh chives but you don't have any, try using finely chopped spring onion.

• Chopped fresh herb stems (such as parsley stalks) are great for adding flavour to soups, sauces and casseroles.

• Keep celery and spring onions fresh for longer by standing them upright with the root ends in a glass of cold water.

• To keep a fresh loaf of bread crusty, store it in a paper or fabric bag. Wrap bread in foil or in a polythene bag if it has a soft crust.

• An excellent way of thickening soups is to stir in a little oatmeal. It adds flavour and richness too.

• If you run out of self-raising flour, sift together 2 level teaspoons of baking powder with every 225 g plain flour. This will not create such a high life as self-raising but it makes a good substitute.

• Bulk out pasta or rice salad by adding a tin of drained and rinsed beans such as chickpeas, red kidney beans or black-eye beans. Alternatively, add some tinned sweetcorn kernels or cooked frozen baby broad beans or peas.

• Add pearl barley to soups and stews to add flavour and texture and create a thickening effect.

• Most vegetables keep best in the refrigerator, but a cool, dark place is also good if you don't have enough fridge space. Potatoes should always be stored in the dark, otherwise they will go green or sprout, making them inedible.

• To yield most juice from a citrus fruit, roll it under the palm of you hand on the work surface first. This also makes squeezing easier. Citrus fruits at room temperature also yield more fruit.

• When you are getting to the end of packets of breakfast cereal such as cornflakes or bran flakes, crush the bits left with a rolling pin, then store them in an airtight jar and use as an alternative to breadcrumbs, for example coating chicken or fish portions.

Using leftovers

• Chop leftover fresh herbs, spoon them into an ice-cube tray, top each portion with a little water and freeze. Once solid, put the cubes in a freezer bag. Seal, label and return to the freezer. Add the frozen herb cubes to soups, casseroles and sauces as needed.

• If you have leftover fresh ginger, cut it into thick slices and freeze in a freezer bag for up to 1 month. Defrost, peel and slice, chop or grate as required.

• Use the water in which ham or gammon has been boiled to cook green vegetables, giving them a lovely flavour. You can also use the cooking liquid as the basis for soup if it is not too salty.

• Make leftover bread into breadcrumbs and store in the freezer for up to 3 months.

• Save the cooking water when boiling or steaming vegetables, and add it to soups, sauces, stocks or gravies to add extra flavour and nutrients.

wine cubes to a freezer bag. The wine cubes can be added to casseroles, stews and gravies for extra flavour.

• Use pastry trimmings to make biscuits. Gently knead in flavourings such as desiccated coconut and Demerara sugar, finely chopped nuts, chopped herbs and grated cheese, or poppyseeds, then cut into small rounds or shapes and bake in a moderate oven until crisp and golden brown.

Quick fixes

• If you add too much salt to a soup or casserole, add one or two peeled potatoes (cut into chunks) to soak up the salt, then continue to cook until tender. Discard the potatoes before serving.

• To ripen an avocado or fruit such as a hard nectarine or peach, put it in a brown paper bag with a banana and keep at room temperature – ethylene released from the banana will hasten the ripening process.

• If you are melting plain chocolate and it seizes (becomes stiff and grainy), it has been overheated. Take it off the heat and stir in 1–2 teaspoons of vegetable oil, a few drops at the time, until the chocolate is smooth. However, if

the chocolate is very scorched it may be unusable.

• If marzipan or almond paste has become hard during storage, seal it in a polythene bag with a slice of fresh bread. The moisture from the bread should restore the marzipan to its pliable state.

• If clear honey (or syrup) hardens during storage, stand the jar in a bowl of hot water for a few minutes or until the honey becomes liquid, rotating the jar occasionally.

• Sometimes moist brown sugar, such as muscovado, becomes hard during storage, due to exposure to air. Add a wedge or two of fresh apple or a slice of fresh bread to the sugar container and the moisture should be restored within a couple of days.

• When baking, use the foil wrappers from blocks of butter or hard margarine to grease cake and loaf tins.

• Make your own flour or sugar shaker by carefully hammering a new nail through the metal lid of a clean, screw-top jar to make several holes. Put some flour or sugar in the jar, replace the lid and you have a shaker ready to use.

• Cooked rice is a potential source of food poisoning. Cool leftovers quickly (ideally within an hour), then store in an airtight container in the refrigerator and use within 24 hours Always reheat cooked cold rice until piping hot.

• Leftover grated cheese such as Cheddar freezes well, but soft cheese such as Brie and most blue cheeses (Stilton is an exception) does not. Grated cheese can be used straight from the freezer.

• Freeze leftover wine in an ice-cube tray. Once solid, transfer the

salads, snacks & sides

couscous tabbouleh

couscous tabbouleh

Using cold water to hydrate couscous allows it to fluff up but still retain an al dente texture. Using couscous in a dish like this means you get all the fresh crispness of a salad, but with the sustaining benefits of a grain.

Put the couscous in a bowl with 250 ml cold water – enough to make the couscous just moist rather than saturated. Leave for 10 minutes or until fluffy. When ready, stir in the spring onions, cucumber, tomatoes, parsley and mint.

To make the lemon dressing, put the lemon juice, garlic and olive oil in a bowl and whisk with a fork. Stir into the salad, add salt and pepper to taste, then serve.

serves
4

Q

V

75 g couscous

4 spring onions,
finely chopped

⅛ cucumber, diced

3 tomatoes (about 300 g),
deseeded and diced

a large handful of fresh flat
leaf parsley, finely chopped

a small handful of fresh mint,
finely chopped

Lemon dressing

juice of 1 lemon

1 garlic clove, crushed

3 tablespoons olive oil

salt and black pepper

Tuscan *tomato* & *bread* salad

This is the perfect thrifty salad – make it when you have the reddest, over-ripe tomatoes and day-old stale bread to use up.

Preheat the oven to 180°C (350°F) Gas 4.

Cut the tomatoes in half, spike with slivers of garlic and roast in the preheated oven for about 1 hour, or until wilted and some of the moisture has evaporated.

Meanwhile, put the bread on an oiled stove-top griddle pan and cook until lightly toasted and barred with grill marks on both sides. Tear or cut the toast into pieces and put into a salad bowl. Sprinkle with a little water until damp. Add the tomatoes, cucumber, onion, parsley, salt and pepper. Sprinkle with the olive oil and vinegar, toss well, then set aside for about 1 hour to develop the flavours.

Add the basil leaves and capers and serve.

serves
4

Q

V

6 very ripe tomatoes

2 garlic cloves, sliced

4 thick slices of day-old bread

about 10 cm cucumber,
halved, deseeded and thinly
sliced

1 red onion, chopped

1 tablespoon freshly chopped
flat leaf parsley

8–12 tablespoons olive oil

2 tablespoons white wine
vinegar or cider vinegar

a handful of fresh basil
leaves, torn

4 tablespoons capers packed
in brine, rinsed and drained

salt and black pepper

60 g bulgur wheat

1 tablespoon lemon juice

1 tablespoon freshly snipped chives

½ yellow pepper, deseeded and diced

8 radishes, sliced

75 g spinach

150 g smoked mackerel fillets, flaked

black pepper

Dressing

3 tablespoons fromage frais

2 teaspoons horseradish sauce

1 teaspoon freshly snipped chives

smoked mackerel & bulgur wheat salad

serves
2

Q

F

The creamy horseradish dressing is a fabulous complement to the richness of the smoked mackerel in this salad, while raw vegetables add crunch and colour.

Cook the bulgur wheat in a saucepan of lightly salted boiling water for 15 minutes or until tender. Drain, then mix with the lemon juice, chives, yellow pepper and radishes.

Divide the spinach leaves between 2 shallow salad bowls, spoon the bulgur wheat on top, then add the flaked smoked mackerel. Mix the dressing ingredients together and drizzle over the fish. Finish with black pepper.

1–2 fat garlic cloves, crushed

1 tablespoon sherry vinegar or white wine vinegar

6 tablespoons olive oil

600 g cooked or tinned cannellini beans, rinsed and drained

2 red onions, thinly sliced into petals (and blanched to take the sharp edge off), or 6 small spring onions, sliced

400 g tinned tuna

salt and black pepper

a handful of fresh basil leaves, torn

tuna & bean salad

serves
6

Q

F

You can usually make this when you come home from work, all the shops have shut, and you've run out of almost everything. Though not quite as good, you can replace the cannellini beans with chickpeas, lentils, borlotti beans and green flageolets, and even use tinned salmon instead of tuna. Easy and adaptable.

Put the garlic on a chopping board, crush with the flat of a knife, add a large pinch of salt, then mash to a paste with the tip of the knife. Transfer to a bowl, add the vinegar and 2 tablespoons of the oil and beat with a fork.

Add the beans and onions and toss gently. Taste, then add extra oil and vinegar to taste.

Drain the tuna and separate into large chunks. Add to the bowl and turn gently to coat with the dressing. Top with the basil and some black pepper.

*smoked mackerel &
bulgur wheat salad*

Greek barley salad

Greek *barley* salad

This hearty version of the traditional and much-loved Greek salad incorporates satisfyingly chewy and filling barley.

Cook the barley in a saucepan of boiling salted water for 30 minutes or until tender. Drain and set aside until needed.

In a large serving bowl, whisk together the lemon juice and zest, vinegar and oil, then stir in the warm barley and mix well. Leave to cool.

Soak the onion in a bowl of iced water for 10 minutes. Drain well.

Add the drained onion to the barley along with the tomatoes, cucumber, green pepper and olives and mix to combine. Season to taste with salt and pepper. Crumble the feta over the top of the salad and sprinkle with oregano. Serve immediately.

serves **4**

V

100 g pearl barley

juice and finely grated zest of 1 unwaxed lemon

2 teaspoons white or red wine vinegar

4 tablespoons olive oil

1 red onion, thinly sliced

4 tomatoes, chopped

1 large cucumber, deseeded and chopped

1 green pepper, deseeded and chopped

20 pitted kalamata olives

150 g feta cheese

1 teaspoon dried oregano

salt and black pepper

green beans in *tomato* sauce

Good served hot or cold, this is stunning in its simplicity. Serve it as a starter or a side.

Put the olive and chilli oils and garlic in a large saucepan and heat until the garlic has turned very lightly golden. Stir in the tomatoes, 250 ml water and a generous pinch of salt. Bring to the boil, then add the beans. Cover with a lid and cook gently for 30–40 minutes, stirring occasionally, until the beans are very tender.

serves **4**

V

4 tablespoons olive oil

1 teaspoon chilli oil

1 garlic clove, crushed

800 g tinned chopped tomatoes

600 g green beans, trimmed

salt

slow-roasted *tomatoes*

6–10 ripe plum tomatoes

2 garlic cloves, finely chopped

1 tablespoon dried oregano

4 tablespoons olive oil

salt and black pepper

fresh basil leaves, to serve

 serves **4**

 V

These firm but juicy tomatoes burst with the flavour of the sun. They take no time to prepare, but need a long time in the oven and smell fantastic while cooking. Plum tomatoes have less moisture and work well, but you can use any tasty variety. It's hard to believe such a simple recipe can be so delicious.

Preheat the oven to 160°C (325°F) Gas 3.

Cut the tomatoes in half lengthways (around the middle if using round tomatoes). Put them cut side up on a baking tray.

Put the garlic, oregano, olive oil, salt and pepper in a bowl and mix well, then spoon or brush the mixture over the cut tomatoes.

Bake in the preheated oven for 1½–2 hours, checking every now and then. The tomatoes should be slightly shrunk but still brilliantly red after cooking (if they are too dark, they will taste bitter). Serve, topped with basil leaves, as an accompaniment to grills and fish, or use on top of bruschetta.

spicy *halloumi* & *chickpeas*

1 tablespoon olive oil

1 onion, finely chopped

1 garlic clove, crushed

1 tablespoon harissa paste (see Note in method)

400 g tinned chickpeas, drained

400 g tinned chopped tomatoes

125 g halloumi cheese, cubed

100 g baby spinach

juice of ½ lemon

salt and black pepper

grated Parmesan, to serve

 serves **2**

 Q

 V

Halloumi has a reasonably long shelf-life before it is opened, which means you can keep a pack tucked away in the fridge. Harissa is a fiery paste – see Note below to make your own.

Put the oil into a large saucepan and gently sauté the onion and garlic until softened. Add the harissa paste, chickpeas and chopped tomatoes. Bring to the boil and simmer for about 5 minutes.

Add the halloumi cheese and spinach, cover and cook over low heat for a further 5 minutes. Season to taste and stir in the lemon juice. Spoon onto serving plates and sprinkle with the Parmesan cheese. Serve immediately with a crisp green side salad.

Note: If you don't have harissa paste, you can make your own by mixing together ½ teaspoon cayenne pepper, 1 tablespoon ground cumin, 1 tablespoon tomato purée and the juice of 1 lime.

slow-roasted tomatoes

tomatoey *green beans* with *onion & fennel seeds*

Spice up your customary boiled green beans with fragrant fennel seeds, onions and a dash of tomato purée.

500 g green beans, trimmed

4 tablespoons olive oil

1 onion, thinly sliced

1 teaspoon fennel seeds, lightly crushed

1 tablespoon tomato purée

salt and black pepper

 serves 4

 Q

V

Bring a saucepan of salted water to the boil and add the beans. Boil for about 6 minutes until tender yet crisp. Meanwhile, heat the olive oil in a frying pan and cook the onion for about 5 minutes until just beginning to colour and soften.

Drain the beans and set aside.

Add the crushed fennel seeds to the onion with plenty of salt and pepper. Mix the tomato purée with 100 ml warm water and add to the onion mixture. Bring to the boil and stir in the beans, tossing well to coat with the sauce. Taste and season again. Cover and simmer gently for 5 minutes, then serve.

cauliflower with *anchovies*

1 dried bay leaf

2 cauliflowers, about 600 g, separated into florets

3–5 tablespoons olive oil

3 long, thin inner celery sticks, finely chopped, plus a handful of leaves, chopped

6 tinned anchovy fillets in oil, chopped

3–4 garlic cloves, finely chopped

juice of ½ lemon

Tabasco sauce (optional)

salt and black pepper

 serves 4

 Q

 F

It can be hard to know what to do with cauliflower to make it tasty or interesting. You don't always want anything as heavy as cauliflower cheese. Try this and you'll be converted.

Bring a large saucepan of water to the boil with the bay leaf. Add a generous amount of salt, then the cauliflower. Cook for 2–3 minutes just to blanch. Drain and set aside.

Heat 3 tablespoons of the oil in a large frying pan. Add the celery stalks and cook for 1 minute. Add the cauliflower and a good pinch of salt and cook for 2–3 minutes over medium-high heat, without stirring.

Add the remaining oil if it needs it (this dish can be slightly oily), then the anchovies, and cook for 2–3 minutes more. Add the garlic, stir well and cook for 30 seconds – do not let the garlic burn. Remove from the heat and stir in the celery leaves. Add the lemon juice and salt and pepper to taste. Add a few drops of Tabasco if you like. Serve hot or at room temperature.

carrots & courgettes with mint

tomatoey green beans with onion & fennel seeds

carrots & courgettes with *mint*

The natural sugars in the vegetables are used in this dish to caramelize and combine with the vinegar. It is normally done quickly in a frying pan, but when cooking in quantity, you can successfully roast them in the oven.

Preheat the oven to 200°C (400°F) Gas 6.

Put half the olive oil in a bowl, add the carrots and toss to coat. Transfer the carrots to a roasting tin and cook in the preheated oven for 15 minutes.

Meanwhile, toss the courgettes in the remaining olive oil, then stir into the carrots when they have cooked for 15 minutes. Roast together for a further 10 minutes until tender and caramelized. Remove from the oven, season with salt and pepper, then add the mint and vinegar to the roasting tin, mixing well.

Set the tin over high heat on top of the stove and let it bubble for a few seconds to reduce the vinegar. Mix well. Serve hot or at room temperature.

serves
4

V

6 tablespoons olive oil

2 courgettes, cut into matchsticks

2 carrots, cut into matchsticks

2 tablespoons wine vinegar

a few sprigs of fresh mint

salt and black pepper

sautéed greens

sautéed *greens*

This method of cooking sprouts and cabbage ensures that they remain crisp and tasty. A great match with pork.

serves 4–6

Q

V

400 g Brussels sprouts

1 tablespoon olive oil

1 tablespoon butter

1 teaspoon caraway seeds

¼ green cabbage, thinly sliced

½ iceberg lettuce, cut into 1-cm slices

juice of ½ lemon

½ teaspoon salt

Separate as many leaves as you can from the sprouts and then finely slice any remaining leaves that are too tight to separate. Set aside.

Heat a large frying pan or wok. Add the oil and butter and heat to medium. Add the caraway seeds and sizzle for about 30 seconds. Add the Brussels sprouts and cabbage and stir-fry for about 4 minutes, or until wilted. Add the lettuce, stir-fry for a further minute, then quickly transfer to a serving dish to stop the cooking.

Pour over the lemon juice and sprinkle with the salt. Toss and serve.

braised *celery*

Poor old celery; it is more often an ingredient than the star of a dish. However, in this recipe, it takes centre stage.

serves 4–6

M

2 whole bunches of celery

2 tablespoons olive oil

75 g bacon lardons

1 onion, sliced

1 carrot, finely chopped

2 garlic cloves, sliced

200 g tinned chopped tomatoes

250 ml dry white wine

1 fresh or dried bay leaf

50 g tinned anchovy fillets, about 8, chopped

a handful of fresh flat leaf parsley, chopped

salt and black pepper

Remove any tough outer stalks from the celery and trim the tips so they will just fit into a large frying pan with a lid.

Bring a large saucepan of water to the boil. Add a pinch of salt, then the celery and simmer gently for 10 minutes to blanch. Remove, drain and pat dry with kitchen paper.

Heat the oil in the frying pan. Add the bacon lardons, onion and carrot and cook gently until lightly browned. Add the celery and a little salt and pepper and cook just to brown, then remove.

Add the garlic, cook for 1 minute, then add the tomatoes, wine and bay leaf. Bring to the boil and cook for 1 minute. Add the celery, cover and simmer gently for 30 minutes, turning the celery once during cooking.

Transfer the celery to a serving dish. Raise the heat and cook the sauce to reduce it slightly, about 10 minutes. Pour it over the celery, sprinkle with the anchovies and parsley and serve.

roasted *vegetable* dauphinois

1 garlic clove

melted butter, for brushing

400 g parsnips, trimmed and cut into 1-cm diagonal slices

a handful of fresh sage leaves

350 g carrots, cut into 1-cm diagonal slices

350 g uncooked beetroot, scrubbed well and cut into 1-cm diagonal slices

275 ml double cream

1 tablespoon olive oil

salt and black pepper

a baking dish, about 30 cm square

serves 4

V

This rich, creamy, garlicky sauce is offset by the earthy flavours of root vegetables, plus the slightly tart and highly aromatic sage. It is incredibly straightforward to prepare and everyone will love it. It's delicious with lamb.

Preheat the oven to 200°C (400°F) Gas 6.

Rub the garlic around the base and sides of the baking dish, then brush with butter. Pack overlapping slices of parsnips into the dish. Season well with salt and pepper, then add one-third of the sage leaves.

Repeat the process, first with the carrots, then the beetroot, seasoning each layer and dotting with the remaining sage. Pour in the cream.

Cover the dish with foil and bake in the preheated oven for about 1 hour 40 minutes. Remove the foil and lightly sprinkle the top with the olive oil. Return to the oven and continue cooking for a further 20 minutes or until the vegetables are very tender.

potatoes en papillote

500 g very small new potatoes

50 g unsalted butter

4 sprigs of fresh herbs, such as thyme, tarragon, chervil, mint or rosemary

1 egg, beaten

salt

serves 4

V

Cooking in a parcel means that all the flavour and goodness of the potatoes is retained as they cook in their own steam. If you're lucky enough to have a glut of new potatoes from your own garden, use them in this simple and delicious side dish.

Preheat the oven to 200°C (400°F) Gas 6.

Cut out 4 sheets of greaseproof or parchment paper, 30 x 38 cm each, and fold in half. Draw a large curve to make a heart shape when unfolded. Cut around the line and open out. Place a quarter of the potatoes on one half of each piece of paper. Dot the butter evenly all over, sprinkle with salt and add a herb sprig to each one.

Brush the edges of the paper lightly with the beaten egg and fold over. Starting from the rounded end, pleat the edges together so that each parcel is completely sealed. Twist the ends together. Put the parcels on a baking tray and cook in the preheated oven for 25–30 minutes, or until the parcels are well puffed and the potatoes are tender. Serve immediately.

roasted vegetable dauphinois

Spanish migas with bacon

Spanish migas with *bacon*

Migas are a Spanish treasure. They are an ancient and original peasant snack – bread simply sprinkled with salted water and fried in olive oil, here with some bacon and chilli.

serves **4**

M

200 g 2-day-old country bread, crusts removed

125 ml olive oil

100 g streaky bacon, diced, or bacon lardons

3 garlic cloves, bruised

1 fat dried red chilli, deseeded and finely chopped

salt

Cut the bread into fingers, spread out on a tea towel, then spray or sprinkle lightly with water and a little salt. Wrap up in the towel and leave for 2 hours. Unwrap the cloth and break the bread into big pieces.

Heat 2 teaspoons of the oil in a frying pan, add the bacon and fry until crisp. Drain on kitchen paper.

Wipe the pan clean and heat the remaining oil. Add the garlic, fry until golden, then remove and discard. Add all the breadcrumbs at once and stir-fry until evenly golden. Stir in the chilli and bacon and serve very hot. Eat with your fingers or little spoons.

butternut squash & *goats' cheese* gratin

A lovely dish, beautifully balanced and perfect for an evening at home with friends. Parsnips and ginger are a surprising combination but the sweetness of the parsnips and the warm flavour of the ginger are compelling and an interesting variation on the traditional mashed potato.

serves **4**

V

2 kg butternut squash or pumpkin, peeled, deseeded and cut into chunks

4 tablespoons olive oil

50 g unsalted butter, chopped

350 g tinned sweetcorn, drained

½ teaspoon grated nutmeg

2 garlic cloves, crushed

a handful of fresh thyme leaves

140 g fresh breadcrumbs

100 g firm goats' cheese, grated

salt and black pepper

Preheat the oven to 200°C (400°F) Gas 6.

Put the squash in a baking dish with 1 tablespoon of the olive oil, the butter, sweetcorn, nutmeg, garlic, thyme and seasoning.

To make the topping, mix the breadcrumbs, goats' cheese and remaining oil in a bowl, then sprinkle over the squash. Cover with foil and bake in the preheated oven for 40 minutes.

Remove the foil and cook for a further 15 minutes until golden brown on top.

falafel

Falafels are very good served with Hoummus (page 44) and a refreshing salad like the Couscous Tabbouleh (page 15).

250 g dried, skinless broad beans, soaked overnight in cold water to cover

1 large onion, about 400 g, chopped

2 garlic cloves, crushed

1 tablespoon ground cumin

1 tablespoon ground coriander

1 teaspoon ground allspice

¼ teaspoon cayenne pepper

¼ teaspoon baking powder

200 g fresh flat leaf parsley

a handful of fresh coriander

groundnut or sunflower oil, for deep-frying

Drain and rinse the beans. Put them in a food processor, then add the onion, garlic, cumin, ground coriander, allspice, cayenne pepper and baking powder. Process to an almost-smooth paste – it should be a little grainy.

Add the parsley and coriander and process briefly again. The greenery should be coarsely chopped and identifiable. (You may have to divide the ingredients in half and process in 2 batches, depending on the size of your processor). Empty into a bowl and set aside for at least 1 hour.

Take 1 tablespoon of the mixture and shape it into a flat round shape, about 5–6 cm in diameter. Continue until all the mixture has been used.

Heat a 1-cm depth of oil in a large non-stick frying pan, add a single layer of the falafels and fry until golden and crisp on one side, then turn them over to crisp on the other side. Remove with a slotted spoon and drain on kitchen paper. Repeat until all the falafels have been fried.

bubble & squeak patties

A great way of using up leftover mashed potatoes, these patties are good with grilled tomatoes and sausages. They're also just as nice eaten cold as a snack.

100 g Savoy cabbage, shredded

250 g potatoes, peeled, cooked and mashed

50 g mature Cheddar, grated

1½ teaspoons Dijon mustard

1 small egg, lightly beaten

plain flour, for dusting

2 tablespoons sunflower or rapeseed oil

salt and black pepper

Steam the cabbage for 2–3 minutes until just tender. Leave to cool, then squeeze out any excess water using your hands.

Finely chop the cabbage, then put it in a bowl with the mashed potatoes, cheese and Dijon mustard. Season to taste and mix until combined, then stir in the egg.

Divide the mixture into 6. Using floured hands, form each portion into a flat round shape. Lightly dust each patty with flour.

Pour the oil into a large non-stick frying pan and heat. Cook 3 patties at a time for 3–4 minutes each side until golden, adding a little more oil if necessary. Remove with a slotted spoon and drain on kitchen paper.

falafel

lemony *mushrooms* on toast

2 tablespoons olive oil

2 dried bay leaves

2 strips of lemon zest

500 g large, flat field mushrooms, thinly sliced

2 garlic cloves, sliced

1 handful of fresh flat leaf parsley, chopped

1 tablespoon lemon juice

4 slices of sourdough bread, lightly toasted

salt and black pepper

serves
4

Try to use meaty field mushrooms here, as they keep their shape when cooked and can hold their own against the quietly intense flavour of bay leaves. This may just be mushroooms on toast, but sometimes the simplest things are the best.

Put the oil in a frying pan and set it over high heat. Add the mushrooms and cook for 8–10 minutes, turning them often. Add the bay leaves and lemon zest to the pan and cook for 1 minute to just flavour the mushrooms. Add the garlic and parsley, stir and cook for 1 minute, making sure that the garlic does not burn. Add the lemon juice and season well.

Spoon the mushroom mixture onto the slices of toasted sourdough bread and serve immediately.

olive oil & *garlic* bruschetta

6 tablespoons olive oil, plus extra for drizzling

4 large garlic cloves, thinly sliced

a good pinch of chilli flakes

4 tablespoons freshly chopped parsley (optional)

4 thick slices of country bread, preferably sourdough

serves
4

This is pared-down simplicity and so easy to make. It beats the likes of doughballs and garlic bread hands down. The most important thing is not to overcook the garlic – it must on no account turn brown. This is great served instead of garlic bread with a selection of salads.

Heat a small pan, pour in the olive oil and stir in the garlic. Cook until the garlic starts to give off its aroma and is golden but not brown (or it will taste bitter). Remove from the heat, then mix in the chilli flakes and parsley, if using. Cover to keep warm.

To make the bruschetta, grill, toast or pan-grill the bread on both sides until lightly charred or toasted, then drizzle with olive oil. Spoon or brush over the garlicky chilli oil.

tomato & *garlic* bruschetta

Traditionally, this Italian peasant dish is just a slice of bread grilled over hot coals, rubbed with garlic and drizzled with olive oil. The ripe tomato is just crushed in your hand and smashed onto the bread, then eaten immediately. This is bruschetta at its simplest and best. This version is more civilized, but you should try the real thing – it's great fun!

Roughly chop the tomatoes and season with salt and pepper.

To make the bruschetta, grill, toast or pan-grill the bread on both sides until lightly charred or toasted. Rub the top side of each slice with the cut garlic, then drizzle with olive oil.

Spoon the tomatoes over the bruschetta and drizzle with more olive oil.

serves
4

Q

V

4 large, very ripe tomatoes

4 thick slices of country bread, preferably sourdough

2 garlic cloves, halved

olive oil, for drizzling

salt and black pepper

olive oil & garlic bruschetta

tomato & garlic bruschetta

bread & accompaniments

chilli cornbread

chilli cornbread

Hearty, quick to make, and satisfying, cornbread is a great accompaniment to have in your cooking repertoire. Toast it to enjoy with a soup, or have it plain with a smattering of butter for a tasty snack.

Preheat the oven to 200°C (400°F) Gas 6.

Sift the flour and baking powder into a mixing bowl and stir in the cornmeal and salt.

Mix the eggs, buttermilk and oil in a second bowl, then, using a wooden spoon, stir into the dry ingredients to make a smooth batter. Stir in the corn, chilli and coriander and pour into the prepared loaf tin.

Bake in the preheated oven for 40 minutes. Leave to cool in the tin for about 5 minutes, then remove from the tin and leave to cool on a wire rack.

serves
8

V

75 g plain flour

1 tablespoon baking powder

200 g medium cornmeal or polenta

1 teaspoon salt

3 eggs, beaten

300 ml buttermilk

4 tablespoons olive oil

200 g tinned sweetcorn, drained

1–2 red chillies, deseeded and chopped

2 tablespoons freshly chopped coriander

a deep loaf tin, 1 kg, greased and base-lined with greaseproof paper

soda bread

This is the classic Irish soda bread made with bicarbonate of soda as the raising agent rather than yeast.

Preheat the oven to 230°C (450°F) Gas 8.

Put the flour, bicarbonate of soda, salt and sugar into a bowl and mix well. Make a well in the centre, add the buttermilk and gradually work it into the flour to make a soft dough.

Knead on a lightly floured surface for 5 minutes and then shape into a flattened round loaf. Transfer to an oiled baking tray and, using a sharp knife, cut a cross in the top of the dough. Sprinkle with a little extra flour.

Bake in the preheated oven for 15 minutes, then reduce the heat to 200°C (400°F) Gas 6 and bake for a further 30 minutes until risen and the loaf sounds hollow when tapped underneath.

Transfer to a wire rack and leave to cool completely.

serves
4

V

400 g wholemeal flour, plus extra for sprinkling

1 teaspoon bicarbonate of soda

1 teaspoon salt

1 teaspoon sugar

300 ml buttermilk

Tuscan *olive* & *rosemary* bread

375 g plain flour

125 g wholemeal flour

1 teaspoon freshly chopped rosemary needles

75 g pitted black and green olives, chopped

1 tablespoon baking powder

½ teaspoon salt

2 large eggs

3 tablespoons olive oil

about 175 ml milk

A rustic loaf flavoured with fresh rosemary, this is good served warm from the oven to accompany winter soups and salads.

Preheat the oven to 180°C (350°F) Gas 4.

Mix the plain and wholemeal flours with the chopped rosemary, olives, baking powder and salt in a large mixing bowl.

In a separate bowl, lightly beat the eggs with the olive oil and milk, then stir into the dry ingredients to make a soft and slightly sticky dough. If there are dry crumbs or the dough feels stiff, work in a little more milk. Turn out the dough onto a lightly floured work surface and shape into a ball about 18 cm across. Set it on a greased baking tray and score the top with a knife.

Bake in the preheated oven for about 45 minutes, or until golden brown and the loaf sounds hollow when tapped underneath. This loaf is best eaten the same day but can be frozen for up to 1 month.

golden *potato* scones

4 rashers of bacon, finely chopped

150–175 g plain flour

2 teaspoons baking powder

½ teaspoon salt

50 g unsalted butter, diced

125 g cooked mashed potato

50 g Parmesan, diced

1 teaspoon dried oregano

about 2 tablespoons milk

1 egg yolk, beaten, to glaze

a 6-cm round, fluted cutter

Use up some leftover mashed potatoes in these little Scottish scones – they help to give the scones a light, moist texture.

Preheat the oven to 220°C (425°F) Gas 7.

Heat a frying pan and dry-fry the bacon for 5–6 minutes, or until crispy. Remove with a slotted spoon and leave to cool on kitchen paper.

Sieve the flour, baking powder and salt together into a large mixing bowl. Add the butter and rub in until the mixture resembles breadcrumbs. Add the potato, Parmesan, oregano and bacon and mix well. Add enough milk to form a soft but firm dough, turn out onto a lightly floured work surface and knead briefly. Roll out the dough to 1.5 cm thick and, using the cutter, stamp out rounds. Re-roll any trimmings and cut more rounds, to make about 10 in total.

Place the scones on a well-greased baking tray, brush the tops with the beaten egg and cook in the preheated oven for 10–15 minutes, or until golden brown and well risen. Serve warm, spread with butter.

serves **4**

V

makes **10**

M

*Tuscan olive &
rosemary bread*

'roof tiles'

Perhaps you made some pizza dough a little while ago, and now you don't know what to do with that leftover Italian flour, or you want to make some ultra-simple and versatile crispbreads to accompany any kind of meal. Here's the recipe you've been after. To ring the changes, flavour the 'roof tiles' by adding dried rosemary or oregano to the flour.

1 tablespoon salt

100 ml warm water

250 g Italian '00' flour

2 tablespoons olive oil

2 large, heavy baking trays

Mix the salt with the warm water until dissolved. Sift the flour into a medium bowl and make a well in the centre. Pour in the salty water and olive oil. Mix well, then knead the dough lightly for a couple of minutes until it is smooth. The dough should be quite firm. Wrap it in clingfilm and leave to rest for 15 minutes.

Preheat the oven to 180°C (350°F) Gas 4.

Divide the dough into 8. Roll or pull the pieces into long ovals. Roll them as thinly as you can (a couple of millimetres) and keep the work surface well floured to prevent sticking. Alternatively you can use a pasta machine to roll them out if you are making a large quantity.

Lay the tiles on the baking trays and prick all over with a fork with large tines. Make sure they are liberally peppered with holes. Bake in the preheated oven for 15–20 minutes, or until evenly pale golden and dried out. Leave to cool on a wire rack and store in an airtight container for up to 2 weeks.

*chopped liver
with zhoug*

4 tablespoons olive oil

1 onion, chopped

500 g chicken livers,
cleaned and trimmed

4 hard-boiled eggs, peeled

salt and black pepper

sweet paprika and matzo
crackers, to serve

Zhoug

1 teaspoon cumin seeds

4 large mild green chillies,
deseeded and chopped

8 tablespoons freshly
chopped flat leaf parsley

8 tablespoons freshly
chopped coriander

1 garlic clove, chopped

125 ml olive oil

chopped *liver* with *zhoug*

serves
4–6

Q

M

Chopped liver with egg makes a simple, loose pâté. The pâté is
perfect served with zhoug, a traditional Jewish fresh herb salsa.

To make the zhoug, heat a small frying pan and toast the cumin seeds for
30 seconds until fragrant. Remove from the heat and crush with a pestle and
mortar. Put in a small food processor with the chillies, parsley, coriander
and garlic and blend to a rough paste, adding the olive oil slowly as you
do so. Season. Store, chilled, in an airtight container for up to 2 weeks.

Heat 2 tablespoons of the olive oil in a large frying pan and sauté the onion
for 6 minutes, or until soft and pale golden. Set aside.

Season the livers. Heat 1 tablespoon of the oil over high heat and cook half
the livers for 3–4 minutes. Set aside and cook the remaining livers. Finely
chop the livers and eggs and combine with the onion, then season. Transfer
to a dish and sprinkle with paprika. Serve with zhoug and matzo crackers.

carrot, orange & cumin dip

carrot, orange & cumin dip

This is an aromatic, tangy dip perfect to serve with vegetable crudités or savoury wafers. You barely need any ingredients so the chances are that you can rustle it up even if your fridge and kitchen cupboards are looking a little bare.

Steam the carrots for 15–20 minutes, or until tender. Meanwhile, heat the olive oil in a frying pan and gently fry the onion, garlic and cumin for 5 minutes, or until softened.

Transfer to a food processor, add the carrots, orange juice and seasoning and blend until smooth. Season to taste and leave to cool. Serve at room temperature with Roof Tiles or other crackers. Store in a screw-top jar in the fridge for up to 2 days.

serves
4–6

Q

V

500 g carrots, chopped

2 tablespoons olive oil

1 small onion, finely chopped

1 garlic clove, chopped

1 teaspoon ground cumin

75 ml orange juice

salt and black pepper

'Roof Tiles' (page 41) or other crackers, to serve

tuna & caramelized onion pâté

3 tablespoons olive oil

3 large onions, thinly sliced

1 tablespoon finely chopped fresh flat leaf parsley

200 g tinned tuna in olive oil

salt and black pepper

toast, to serve

This delicate pâté relies on getting as much flavour as possible out of slow-cooked onions, and the quality of a few simple ingredients, which you are bound to have sitting in your kitchen cupboards – tinned tuna, olive oil and onions. Hopefully, there will be some fresh or frozen parsley to be found too to make this pâté that little bit more special.

Heat the olive oil in a large, heavy-based saucepan over very low heat. Add the onions and cook gently for 1 hour, stirring occasionally, until the onions are very soft and just turning golden. Remove from the heat.

Mix together the onions, parsley and tuna, with its preserving oil, and season to taste. For a smoother pâté, process the ingredients in a food processor. Transfer to a serving dish and serve with toast.

hoummus

175 g dried chickpeas, soaked in cold water overnight, or 800 g tinned chickpeas

2 tablespoons tahini paste

2 garlic cloves, chopped

juice of 1–2 lemons

1 tablespoon ground cumin

2 tablespoons olive oil

300 ml chickpea cooking liquid

salt and black pepper

To serve

1 tablespoon olive oil

1 tablespoon finely chopped fresh coriander

pitta bread, toast, or 'Roof Tiles' (page 41), to serve

It's tempting to buy ready-made hoummus but it's so easy to make and nothing beats the fresh, home-made kind. You can use dried chickpeas, which will need to soak overnight, or tinned chickpeas for speed.

Drain and rinse the soaked chickpeas and put them in a saucepan. Cover with plenty of water, bring to the boil and skim until clear. Cover and cook until perfectly soft, about 1 hour.

Strain the chickpeas, reserving the cooking liquid. If using tinned chickpeas, strain them first and discard the liquid, but use about 4 tablespoons cold water in the food processor.

If the tahini paste appears separated in the jar, mix it properly first. Divide all the ingredients into 2 batches and put the first batch in a food processor, then process briefly. Ideally it should still have some texture and should not be too solid. Taste and adjust the seasoning, then blend again briefly. Transfer to a bowl and repeat with the remaining ingredients.

Trickle a little oil over the top and sprinkle with fresh coriander. Serve at room temperature with pitta bread, toast or Roof Tiles.

tuna & caramelized onion pâté

spicy *tomato, black bean & feta* dip

The fresh flavours in this Tex-Mex-style dip seem to have a natural affinity with corn chips. This is a twist on the popular chilli con queso (chilli with cheese), usually made with Cheddar or mozzarella. The flavour of Cheddar can be too overpowering and the texture a little greasy with the mildly spiced flavours here, so this recipe calls for feta instead. It doesn't entirely melt, but softens and adds a salty bite to the dip, which enhances the sweetness of the tomatoes and pepper. If you are in a hurry, you can easily substitute the dried beans with tinned red kidney beans.

serves
4

V

90 g dried black beans

1 tablespoon olive oil

1 small red pepper, deseeded and thinly sliced

1 red onion, thinly sliced

1 teaspoon ground cumin

2 garlic cloves, finely chopped

2 small red chillies, finely chopped

3 tomatoes, chopped

1 tablespoon red wine vinegar

250 ml passata

200 g feta cheese, crumbled

corn chips, to serve

Soak the black beans in cold water overnight. Drain and rinse well. Put them in a large saucepan with plenty of water and bring to the boil. Cook for 25–30 minutes, until soft to the bite. Drain well and set aside.

Heat the oil in a saucepan set over high heat and add the red pepper and onion. Reduce the heat to low, cover and cook for about 8 minutes. Add the cumin, garlic and chillies and cook for a further 2 minutes. Add the beans, tomatoes, vinegar and passata and bring to the boil. Reduce the heat and simmer rapidly for about 10 minutes, until almost all the liquid has evaporated and the tomatoes start to look mushy.

Preheat the grill to high.

Transfer the bean mixture to a flameproof dish and sprinkle the crumbled feta over the top. Cook under the hot grill until the cheese is soft and just starting to brown. Serve hot with corn chips on the side for dipping.

bread sauce

300 ml milk

¼ onion, peeled

6 cloves

1 fresh bay leaf

75 g day-old bread, crumbled

15 g unsalted butter

ground nutmeg, to dust

salt and black pepper

A traditional family favourite and much loved way of using up slightly stale bread, this satisfying sauce is infused with cloves and bay leaves for a wonderfully aromatic finish. Although traditionally served with roast turkey, bread sauce is also great with your Sunday roast chicken.

Pour the milk into a saucepan. Stud the onion with the cloves and add to the pan with the bay leaf and a little seasoning. Heat very gently until the milk reaches boiling point, then remove from the heat and set aside to infuse for 20 minutes.

Discard the onion and bay leaf and return the pan to the heat. Add the bread and butter and stir over low heat until the sauce thickens and becomes smooth. (You can purée the sauce with a hand blender if you prefer.) Season to taste and serve dusted with nutmeg.

tahini, yoghurt & *garlic* sauce

250 g Greek yoghurt

1 garlic clove, crushed

1½ tablespoons tahini

1 tablespoon lemon juice

salt and black pepper

Here tahini, made from ground sesame seeds, helps to flavour yoghurt and results in a great accompaniment to roasted or barbecued vegetables, or grilled lamb.

Combine the yoghurt, garlic, tahini and lemon juice in a bowl and season to taste. Cover and set aside to infuse for 30 minutes before serving. Store, chilled, in a screw-top jar for up to 3 days.

bagna cauda

bagna cauda

Made from storecupboard essentials, this warm anchovy butter is best served with an assortment of fresh summer vegetables – just let everyone help themselves.

Heat the butter and garlic together in a small saucepan and cook very gently for 4–5 minutes, or until softened but not browned. Add the anchovies, stir well, then pour in the olive oil. Cook gently for a further 10 minutes, stirring occasionally until the sauce has softened and is almost creamy. Serve warm.

serves
4–6

50 g unsalted butter

4 large garlic cloves, crushed

50 g anchovy fillets in oil, drained and chopped

200 ml olive oil

soups

beef stock

beef stock

Fresh stocks, stock cubes and powders are invaluable, but home-made stocks are infinitely better. Use them in soups, stews and to reduce into sauces. The great thing is that you can make them with the bones left over after roasting a joint, and make a large quantity to freeze and use as and when you need it. This makes about 2 litres.

Put all the ingredients in a large stockpot, cover with 4 litres water and bring to the boil. Reduce the heat to a simmer. For the first 30 minutes, you must skim off the foam that rises to the surface. This will help make the stock clearer and less fatty. It should be just hot enough to let a large, slow bubble break on the surface of the liquid. Do not let it boil, or the fat will be constantly redistributed through the stock. Remove from the heat and strain through a colander into a large bowl. Discard the solids. Leave the stock to cool, then cover and chill overnight.

The next morning, scrape off the fat that has risen to the top. Strain through a fine sieve, then ladle into conveniently sized containers: 1 litre will serve 4 people. If you are left with a little stock that's not enough for a whole recipe, pour it into ice cube trays, freeze, then keep in freezer bags – whenever you need 'a tablespoon of stock', use 1 cube.

M

2 kg beef bones

3 tablespoons unsalted butter or oil (not olive oil) or a mixture of both

500 g stewing beef, cut into 2-cm cubes

2 large onions, chopped

2 large carrots, chopped

a small handful of fresh parsley, stalks bruised

1 tablespoon black peppercorns, lightly crushed

1 leek, split in 4 lengthways, then coarsely chopped

2 celery sticks, thinly sliced

1 bouquet garni (a bunch of herbs tied up with kitchen string)

chicken stock

Chicken stock was traditionally made using an old boiling fowl, full of flavour. These are almost impossible to find these days, and the next best things are kosher chickens, chicken carcasses, chicken wings or drumsticks. This makes about 2 litres.

Put all the ingredients in a large stockpot, add 3 litres cold water and bring to the boil. As the water heats, skim off the foam from time to time. Reduce to simmering and cook, uncovered, for at least 4 hours. Skim off the foam as it accumulates on the surface. Strain through a colander into a bowl. Leave the stock to cool, then cover and chill overnight.

Next morning, scrape off the fat that has risen to the top. Strain through a fine sieve and store as above.

M

2 kg chicken carcasses, or a whole chicken

2 onions, chopped

2 carrots, chopped

1 celery stick, chopped

a few sprigs of fresh parsley, stalks bruised

2 tablespoons black peppercorns, lightly crushed

1 fresh bay leaf, or ½ dried

1 leek, split in 4 lengthways, then coarsely chopped

fish stock

F

Most fishmongers will sell you fish frames and heads. Do not use any oily fish, such as mackerel, tuna, bonito, salmon or trout. You mustn't let the bones boil for more than 30 minutes or they will make the stock gluey. This makes about 1 litre.

75 g unsalted butter

2 onions, cut into wedges

1 carrot, chopped

1 small celery stick, very finely chopped

1 teaspoon black peppercorns

1 small leek, split lengthways, then chopped

1 bouquet garni (a bunch of herbs tied up with kitchen string)

a garlic clove, peeled

150 ml white wine

2 kg white fish trimmings (gills removed)

Melt the butter in a stockpot, add the onions, carrot, celery and peppercorns and cook gently until softened and translucent. Don't let them brown. Add the bouquet garni, garlic and wine and bring to the boil, then add 1 litre iced water and ice cubes. The butter will stick to the ice cubes and you can remove them. Add the fish trimmings, bring to the boil again, reduce the heat and simmer for 30 minutes, skimming occasionally. Remove from the heat and strain out the solids. Strain again through a fine sieve.

Return the strained stock to the rinsed-out saucepan and return to the boil. Simmer until reduced by about a third or a half, to intensify the flavour. Use immediately, or leave to cool, then store as on page 53.

vegetable stock

V

Go easy on highly flavoured items like celery or fennel and omit floury vegetables like potatoes, and any member of the cabbage family, which can become sour. This makes about 1 litre.

2 garlic cloves, crushed

1 large onion, chopped

3 large leeks, halved lengthways, then chopped

2 large carrots, chopped

2 celery sticks, chopped

40 g unsalted butter, melted

1 tablespoon olive oil

a handful of fresh parsley stalks, bruised

1 dried bay leaf

a sprig of fresh thyme

250 ml white wine

Preheat the oven to 200°C (400°F) Gas 6.

Put the garlic, onion, leeks, carrots, butter and olive in a roasting tin and toss until evenly coated. Roast in the preheated oven for 40–45 minutes, turning them from time to time. Transfer the vegetables to a stockpot and put the empty tin on top of the stove. Add the herbs, wine and 500 ml water and scrape up any residues from the tin. Pour into the stockpot. Add 2.5 litres cold water and bring to the boil. Reduce the heat, cover with a lid and simmer for 1 hour. Remove from the heat and leave to cool.

Strain the stock through a fine sieve and discard the vegetables and flavourings. Pour the stock back into the rinsed pan and bring to the boil. Keep boiling until reduced by half. Use immediately, or leave to cool, then store as on page 53.

fish stock

pea, smoked ham
& mint soup

pea, smoked ham & mint soup

Frozen or fresh peas make a very satisfying sweet and savoury base for a soup. If you are into podding your own peas from the garden, the results will be even better, but frozen peas pulled out of the freezer are just as good for a standby supper.

Heat the olive oil in a large saucepan over low heat and add the spring onions. Cook for 2–3 minutes, then add the garlic, ham and half the mint and cook for a further 2 minutes, stirring. Stir in the peas and pour in the hot stock. Simmer for 2–3 minutes until the peas are tender.

Transfer a third of the soup to a blender and liquidize until completely smooth. Pour back into the soup and mix until amalgamated. Season with just a little salt (the ham will be quite salty already) and some black pepper. Add the remaining mint. Serve with more black pepper.

serves 4

Q

M

3 tablespoons olive oil

6 spring onions, chopped

2 garlic cloves, sliced

200 g thick slices of smoked ham, finely chopped

10 g fresh mint, leaves only, or 1 teaspoon dried mint

500 g peas (defrosted or fresh)

1 litre hot Chicken Stock (page 53) or Vegetable Stock (page 54)

salt and black pepper

split pea & sausage soup

Where does a casserole stop and a soup start? This thick wintry mix of tender lentils with chunks of sausage is so filling, it's perfect winter's fare. Roaring fire optional.

Heat the olive oil in a large saucepan and cook the onion, leek and celery gently over low heat for 8–10 minutes. Add the nutmeg and stir in. Add the split peas and mix into the vegetables. Add the stock and bay leaves, cover and simmer for 45 minutes or until the peas are tender and beginning to get mushy when pressed with the back of a spoon.

Meanwhile, grill the sausages until cooked, then roughly chop. Add to the soup and cook for a further 10 minutes. Season to taste and serve.

serves 6

M

2 tablespoons olive oil

1 onion, chopped

1 leek, chopped

2 celery sticks, chopped

a pinch of grated nutmeg

300 g yellow split peas

1.5 litres hot Chicken Stock (page 53)

2 dried bay leaves

250 g sausages

salt and black pepper

chicken, garlic & watercress soup

3 whole garlic bulbs

a 300-g baking potato

900 ml hot Chicken Stock
(page 53)

leftovers from a roasted
chicken, pulled off the
carcass

150 g watercress

salt and black pepper

serves
4

M

If you've had a roast (providing you haven't picked every last bit of meat from it), this is a great way to use up that fantastic meat. There's nothing more satisfying than two meals from one bird; it makes one feel very thrifty and clever.

Preheat the oven to 200°C (400°F) Gas 6.

Wrap the garlic bulbs and potato in foil individually and put in a roasting dish. Roast in the preheated oven for 1 hour.

Open the packages of roasted garlic and potato to allow them to cool off and at the same time check that they are really soft inside. If not, return to the oven for a little longer until soft.

Pour the chicken stock into a large saucepan. Discard the skin from the potato, chop the flesh and add it to the pan. Cut the tops off the garlic bulbs, squeeze out the soft flesh from inside the cloves and add to the soup. Chop up the chicken meat and add that to the soup too. Transfer about a third of the soup to a blender along with the watercress and liquidize until smooth. Return to the pan and stir until blended. Add more water if you think it's too thick. Season to taste and serve.

chicken noodle soup

1 tablespoon olive oil

1 onion, chopped

2 large carrots, chopped

2 celery sticks, thickly sliced

1 litre hot Chicken Stock
(page 53)

90 g fine Jewish egg noodles,
broken into pieces

leftovers from a roasted
chicken, pulled off the
carcass

a small handful of fresh flat
leaf parsley, finely chopped

salt and black pepper

serves
4

Q

M

You really need a deep, flavoursome base for the ultimate chicken noodle soup so only make this with your own chicken stock from page 53. Fine Jewish egg noodles are classic additions to the soup, but you can try rice or matzo balls.

Heat the olive oil in a saucepan. Add the onion, carrots and celery, and season. Sauté for 5 minutes, then pour in the stock. Bring to the boil and add the noodles. Cook until the noodles are al dente.

Chop up the chicken meat, then add to the saucepan. Sprinkle in the chopped parsley, season to taste and serve.

chicken, garlic &
watercress soup

chicken avgolemono

chicken avgolemono

A light, lemony Greek soup – perfect for using up leftover cooked chicken.

serves 4

Q

M

Heat the stock in a large saucepan and add the rice. Bring to the boil and simmer for 15 minutes or until the rice is tender. Add the chicken and warm through for 2–3 minutes.

In the meantime, whisk the eggs with the lemon juice in a small bowl. Add a ladleful of the warm stock and whisk until thinned. Remove the soup from the heat and gradually pour in the egg mixture, whisking to amalgamate it. It should thicken in the residual heat, but if you need to, place it over low heat for just 3–4 minutes, stirring the bottom of the pan to thicken. Do not return to high heat once the egg has been added, or it will boil and scramble. Serve garnished with parsley and croutons.

1.4 litres hot Chicken Stock (page 53)

100 g long-grain rice

400 g cooked chicken, shredded

3 eggs

juice of 1 lemon

freshly chopped flat leaf parsley, to serve

croutons, to serve

French *onion* soup

Here's one of the tastiest soups you're ever likely to enjoy, made with the humblest ingredients. A French culinary triumph.

serves 4–6

M

Put the butter and oil in a large saucepan and heat until the butter melts. Add the onions and salt and stir well. Cook over low heat for 20–30 minutes or until the onions are golden brown. Sprinkle the flour over the onions and stir for 2–3 minutes until there is no sign of white specks of flour.

Pour 1–2 ladles of the hot stock onto the onions. Stir well, then add the remaining stock and simmer, part-covered, for another 20–30 minutes. Season to taste. Meanwhile, preheat the oven to 170°C (325°F) Gas 3.

Put the bread on a baking tray and toast in the preheated oven for about 15 minutes. Brush with the olive oil and rub with the cut garlic clove, return to the oven for another 15 minutes or until the bread is quite dry.

Ladle the soup into 4–6 heatproof soup bowls. Put the slices of toast on top and pile the cheese over them. Dot with more butter and cook at the same temperature for about 15 minutes until the cheese has melted. Put under a preheated grill to brown the top for 1–2 minutes if you like.

50 g unsalted butter, plus extra to finish

1 tablespoon olive oil

1 kg onions, thinly sliced

1 teaspoon salt

50 g plain flour

1 litre hot Beef Stock (page 53), or Beef and Chicken mixed (page 53)

salt and black pepper

To finish

8–12 thick slices of bread (about 2 cm)

1 tablespoon olive oil

1 large garlic clove, halved

125 g Gruyère cheese, grated

tomato soup

1 kg very ripe red tomatoes

500 ml hot Chicken Stock
(page 53), or to taste

salt and black pepper

To serve (optional)

grated zest and juice of
1 unwaxed lemon

4 tablespoons pesto

freshly snipped chives
or torn basil

Keep this simple and fresh with the reddest, ripest tomatoes you can find. Or you can pep it up with a dollop of flavoursome pesto on top before serving.

To skin the tomatoes, cut a cross in the base of each and dunk into a saucepan of boiling water. Remove after 10 seconds and put into a strainer set over a large saucepan. Slip off and discard the skins and cut the tomatoes in half around their 'equators'. Using a teaspoon, deseed into the strainer, then press the pulp and juice through the strainer and add to the blender. Discard the seeds. Chop the tomato halves and add to the blender.

Purée the tomatoes, adding a little of the stock to help the process – you may have to work in batches. Add the remaining stock, season to taste and transfer to the saucepan. Heat well without boiling. Serve topped with a spoonful of lemon juice, lemon zest, pesto, chives or basil, if using, and a little more pepper.

chickpea, lemon & mint soup

1.2 kg tinned chickpeas

2 garlic cloves, crushed

grated zest and juice of
2 unwaxed lemons

3 tablespoons freshly
chopped mint

2 tablespoons olive oil

salt and black pepper

This storecupboard-based soup couldn't be easier. It's made from a minimal number of ingredients, but has an intriguingly complex flavour.

Drain the liquid from the chickpeas into a jug, and make up to 750 ml with water. Tip two-thirds of the drained chickpeas into a food processor add the garlic, lemon zest and juice, mint, olive oil and enough of the chickpea liquid to blend to a purée.

Pour into a saucepan and stir in the remaining whole chickpeas and liquid. Season to taste and heat through for about 5 minutes until gently bubbling. Ladle into bowls and serve immediately.

tomato soup

Swedish *yellow pea* soup

This is a version of a hearty Scandinavian soup. Often, it has no meat in it and uses celeriac instead. So if you want to make this soup vegetarian-friendly, halve a celeriac, peel it and cut into cubes, adding at the same time as the peas. Having said that, this soup really does benefit from being made with smoked pork knuckle, available from butchers. Some Scandinavian cookbooks tell you to soak the peas overnight. You can if you like, but since they're split, they have no coating to be softened. If you can't find yellow split peas in your supermarket, try an Indian one and buy yellow channa dhaal, but not the oiled ones.

serves
4

1 smoked pork knuckle or ham hock

500 g yellow split peas

2 onions, halved lengthways

6 cloves

1 carrot, thickly sliced

3 fresh bay leaves

3 long curls of orange zest

4 tablespoons Dijon mustard

salt (optional – see method) and black pepper

freshly snipped chives or parsley, to serve

Put the pork knuckle in a snug-fitting saucepan and cover it with cold water. Bring to the boil, reduce the heat and simmer until tender. Skim it from time to time and top up with more boiling water as necessary. When done, the meat will fall easily off the bone. Drain, remove the skin and bone and pull the meat into bite-sized shreds, small enough to fit easily on a soup spoon. Reserve 250 ml of the cooking liquid.

Rinse the peas in cold running water and put in a large saucepan. Stud the onions with the cloves. Add the onions, carrot, bay leaves, orange zest and 1 litre water to the saucepan. Bring to the boil, reduce the heat and simmer until done, about 30 minutes.

The peas should be soft, but still keep their shape. If not, cook for a further 5–10 minutes – the time will depend on the age of the peas. Remove the cloves, bay leaves, orange zest and (optional) the onions and carrot. If you would like a smoother texture, the peas can be puréed in a blender or food processor, in batches if necessary.

Return the peas to the saucepan, stir in the mustard and pork shreds and taste for seasoning. Instead of salt, I like to add a little of the reserved liquid used to cook the pork. It will be salty and meaty – take care, it's easy to add too much. Serve sprinkled with herbs.

mixed *bean* soup

serves 4

Q

M/V

Using tinned beans, this soup takes no time at all to prepare, and you can use vegetable or chicken stock, according to whether your audience is vegetarian or not.

1 tablespoon olive oil

3 large garlic cloves, 2 cut into slices, 1 crushed

1 large onion, finely chopped

250 g Puy lentils

1 litre boiling Chicken (page 53) or Vegetable Stock (page 54), plus extra to taste

100 g tinned butter beans

200 g tinned green flageolet beans

200 g tinned red kidney beans

200 g tinned haricot or cannellini beans

salt and black pepper

fresh parsley or basil

Heat the oil in a frying pan, add the sliced garlic and fry gently on both sides until crisp and golden. Remove and drain on kitchen paper.

Add the onion and crushed garlic to the frying pan, adding extra oil if necessary, and cook gently until softened and transparent. Add the lentils and half the boiling stock and cook until the lentils are just tender.

Meanwhile, rinse and drain all the beans. Put them in a sieve and dunk the sieve in a large saucepan of boiling water. The beans are cooked – you are just reheating them.

Add the hot beans to the lentils and add the remaining stock. Season to taste. If the soup is too thick, add boiling stock or water. Ladle into bowls, top with the reserved fried garlic and herbs and serve with crusty bread.

dried pea & spelt soup

serves 4

M/V

Make your own farro (spelt) soup mixture from whatever you have in your cupboard collection of dried peas, beans, lentils, and grains. Spelt, the major grain in the mix, is a very ancient wheat, and is said to be more acceptable to those who are wheat intolerant. Some people prefer barley or other grains.

2–4 tablespoons olive oil

1 carrot, finely chopped

1 onion, chopped

1–2 garlic cloves, crushed

500 g farro mixture (see Note)

1 dried bay leaf

1 litre hot Chicken (page 53) or Vegetable Stock (page 54)

salt and black pepper

grated cheese, to serve

Heat the olive oil in a large saucepan, add the carrot and onion and cook slowly until softened but not browned. Add the garlic and cook until softened. Add the farro mixture, bay leaf and stock and bring to the boil. Simmer slowly until done, about 30 minutes. Season after 20 minutes. Ladle into soup bowls, then serve with a a bowl of grated cheese for people to add themselves.

Note: To make your own mixture, use 200 g farro (spelt) or pearl barley, 100 g yellow split peas, 100 g green split peas and 100 g baby white beans (fagiolini). Soak the baby beans overnight in cold water before using.

mixed bean
soup

carrot & lentil soup

spicy red vegetable soup

carrot & lentil soup

You'll need to use a variety of lentil here that will soften to a mush when cooked for a short time. Orange or red varieties are what's needed and they also help to create the autumnal colour. The taste of this soup belies the simplicity of its ingredients. For a simple twist, try adding a couple of tablespoons of curry powder to the onions at the early stage of cooking.

serves
4

M

3 tablespoons unsalted butter

1 red onion, chopped

1 garlic clove, chopped

2 tablespoons sun-dried tomato purée

500 g carrots, grated

250 g red lentils, rinsed and drained

1.5 litres hot Chicken Stock (page 53)

125 ml natural yoghurt

a handful of fresh coriander leaves, chopped

Heat the butter in a heavy-based saucepan over high heat. When the butter is sizzling, add the onion and garlic and cook for 4–5 minutes, stirring often. Add the sun-dried tomato purée and stir-fry for 1 minute. Add the carrots, lentils and stock to the pan and bring to the boil. Cook at a rapid simmer for 40 minutes, until the lentils are soft.

Spoon the soup, in batches, into a food processor or blender and process until smooth. Return the soup to a clean saucepan and cook over low heat for a few minutes, until heated through. Serve with dollops of yoghurt and the coriander sprinkled on top.

spicy red vegetable soup

The colour of this fiery red vegetable soup is matched by a chilli kick, which can be adjusted according to your palate. It's a really rewarding recipe so don't be put off by the cooking time – use it as an opportunity to put your feet up and relax.

serves
4

V

60 ml light olive oil

1 tablespoon light brown soft sugar

1 red pepper, deseeded and chopped

1 kg tomatoes, quartered

1 red onion, chopped

1 large red chilli, deseeded and chopped

2 garlic cloves, chopped

250 ml hot Vegetable Stock (page 54)

4 slices of rye bread

50 g soft goats' cheese

Preheat the oven to 180°C (350°F) Gas 4.

Put the olive oil, sugar, pepper, tomatoes, onion, chilli and garlic in a roasting tin, toss and cook in the preheated oven for 2 hours, stirring often, until the vegetables are really soft and starting to turn brown.

Remove the vegetables from the oven. Put the stock in a saucepan and stir in the vegetables. Spoon the mixture, in batches, into a food processor or blender and process until smooth. Return the soup to a clean saucepan and cook over low heat for a few minutes until heated through. Toast the rye bread and, while it's still warm, spread over the cheese. Float the toast on top of the soup to serve.

750 g pork belly, sliced

100 g pickling salt

1 onion, peeled

1 clove

1 fresh bay leaf

1 cabbage

1 inner celery stick with leaves, cut into chunks

7 carrots, cut into chunks

4 turnips, cut into chunks

1 tablespoon unsalted butter, plus more for serving

750 g small new potatoes, peeled

salt and black pepper

cabbage soup

serves
4–6

M

A classic case of less is more. This soup is soothing and restorative, and deliciously delicate, despite its rustic origins. Home-made salt pork makes all the difference to the taste and is very simple to make. You will have to sacrifice some fridge space for 3 days, which is the only complication, but you will be well rewarded. Your butcher should be able to supply the salt. If you don't have time to salt the pork yourself, buy a smoked pork knuckle from the butcher and proceed as in the recipe.

Three days before you plan to serve the soup, put the pork belly slices in a shallow ceramic or glass dish and add water to cover. Add the salt and stir until dissolved. Cover and refrigerate for 3 days, turning occasionally. Alternatively, have the butcher salt the pork belly for you.

The day of serving, remove the pork belly from its brine and rinse. Put the pork and onion, studded with the clove, in a large saucepan with 3 litres water. Bring to the boil and skim off any foam that rises to the surface.

Meanwhile, bring another saucepan of water to the boil with a bay leaf. When it boils, add the cabbage and blanch for 5 minutes. Remove the cabbage and drain. When cool enough to handle, slice the cabbage.

Add the sliced cabbage, celery, carrots, turnips and butter to the pork. Taste for seasoning; it may not even need salt because of the salt pork. Return to the boil, then lower the heat, cover and simmer for about 30 minutes. Taste for seasoning again.

Add the potatoes and cook until they are tender, 20–25 minutes more. To serve, remove the pork belly and cut into bite-sized pieces. Trim off any rind and discard any bones. Return the pork pieces to the soup and serve hot, with a spoonful of butter in each bowl and thick slices of country bread.

fennel, leek & cauliflower soup

This deceptively creamy soup doesn't actually contain cream!
It's really just a fancy vegetable soup (which can be made with
either chicken or vegetable stock) but it looks and tastes good
enough for a special meal with guests. Try to buy the vegetables
fresh from a market if at all possible – it will make the soup all
the better.

serves
6

M/V

2 tablespoons olive oil

25 g unsalted butter

2 leeks, sliced

1 large or 2 small bulbs of
fennel, trimmed and sliced
(reserve the feathery leaves to
garnish)

1 large garlic clove, crushed

1 small or ½ large cauliflower

1 litre hot Chicken Stock
(page 53) or Vegetable Stock
(page 54)

1 dried bay leaf

2–3 sprigs fresh tarragon or
1 teaspoon dried tarragon

2–3 tablespoons whole milk
(optional)

a small pinch of mace

salt and black pepper

a few fresh chives, to garnish

Heat the oil for a minute or two in a large saucepan, then add the butter.
When the foaming dies down, add the leeks, fennel and garlic, stir well,
cover and cook over low heat for about 8–10 minutes. Meanwhile, remove
the florets from the cauliflower. Add them to the pan, stir and cook for
another 3–4 minutes. Pour the stock over the vegetables, add the bay leaf
and tarragon and bring to the boil. Partially cover the pan and simmer for
about 15 minutes or until the cauliflower and fennel are soft. Remove from
the heat and leave to cool slightly. Remove the bay leaf and tarragon.
Strain the soup, reserving the liquid.

Put the vegetables in food processor and whizz until smooth, adding
as much of the reserved liquid as you need to make a smooth, creamy
consistency. Whizz the remaining liquid in the blender or food processor
to pick up the last scraps of vegetable purée and add to the soup in the pan.
Reheat gently, diluting the soup with a little more stock or milk if it seems
too thick. Season to taste with salt, pepper and mace.

Chop the reserved fennel leaves and chives into lengths and scatter over
the soup before serving.

Swiss chard & white bean soup

2 tablespoons unsalted butter

1 onion, chopped

a small bunch of Swiss chard (about 350 g), finely chopped

400 g tinned cannellini beans, drained but not rinsed

1 litre hot Vegetable Stock (page 54)

4 thick slices of toast

2 garlic cloves, halved

olive oil, for drizzling

salt and black pepper

grated Parmesan, to serve

2 tablespoons olive oil

2 onions, diced

1 kg butternut squash, peeled, deseeded and chopped

1 garlic clove, crushed

1.2 litres hot Vegetable Stock (page 54)

salt and black pepper

single cream, to serve

Swiss chard & white bean soup

serves 4

Q

V

This minestrone-type soup is beefed up by serving ladles of it over thick and garlicky toast to mop up all the goodness.

Melt the butter in a saucepan over medium heat. Add the onion and cook for 4–5 minutes to soften. Add the Swiss chard and cook for 5 minutes, stirring often, until softened. Mash the beans with a fork, then add to the saucepan with the stock and gently bring to the boil. Season. Rub the bread with the cut side of the garlic, then place each one in a serving bowl. Drizzle each piece of bread with olive oil and ladle over the soup. Sprinkle the Parmesan on top and serve immediately.

golden *butternut squash* soup

serves 4

V

Squash is a wonderfully versatile vegetable, and it's used to great effect in this flavoursome soup.

Heat the oil in a large saucepan, add the squash, onions and garlic and sauté over low heat for 10 minutes. Add the stock, bring to the boil, then simmer for 30 minutes. Using a handheld blender, blitz the soup until smooth and creamy. Season and serve with a drizzle of cream.

golden butternut squash soup

lentil, spinach & cumin soup

Crispy fried onions are a lovely topping on this spiced vegetable soup, but you have to be brave and really brown them so they look almost black. In order to do this without burning them, you have to really soften them to start with. Don't be tempted to leave them out – they really complement the finished soup.

Heat the olive oil in a large, heavy-based saucepan and add the onions. Cook, covered, for 8–10 minutes until softened. Remove half the onion and set aside.

Continue to cook the onion left in the pan for a further 10 minutes until deep brown, sweet and caramelized. Take out and set aside for the garnish.

Return the softened onion to the pan, add the garlic, coriander, cumin seeds and lentils and stir for 1–2 minutes until well coated in oil. Add the stock, bring to the boil, then turn down to a gentle simmer for 30 minutes until the lentils are lovely and soft.

Add the spinach and stir until wilted. Transfer half the soup to a blender and liquidize until you have a purée. Stir back into the soup. Season with lemon juice, salt and black pepper.

To serve, add a dollop of Greek yoghurt and scatter the pine nuts and fried onions over the top.

3 tablespoons olive oil

2 onions, sliced

4 garlic cloves, sliced

1 teaspoon ground coriander

1 teaspoon cumin seeds

150 g brown or green lentils

1.2 litres hot Vegetable Stock (page 54)

200 g spinach

juice of 1 lemon

salt and black pepper

4 tablespoons Greek yoghurt

25 g pine nuts, lightly toasted in a dry frying pan

la ribollita

serves
8

V

250 g dried cannellini beans

150 ml olive oil

1 onion, finely chopped

1 carrot, chopped

1 celery stick, chopped

2 leeks, finely chopped

4 garlic cloves, finely chopped, plus 1 extra, peeled and bruised, for rubbing

1 small white cabbage, thinly sliced

1 large potato, chopped

4 courgettes, chopped

400 ml tomato passata

2 sprigs of fresh rosemary

2 sprigs of fresh thyme

2 sprigs of fresh sage

1 dried red chilli

500 g cavolo nero or Savoy cabbage, finely sliced

6 thick slices of coarse crusty white bread

salt and black pepper

grated Parmesan, to serve

There's nothing quite like a huge plate of thick, warming Italian ribollita on a damp autumn evening beside a crackling, scented log fire. Best made in large quantities, this is a great soup for a family get-together and is very filling. Ribollita means 'reboiled', and is made from whatever vegetables are around, but must contain beans and the delicious Tuscan black winter cabbage, cavolo nero. Savoy cabbage makes a good alternative. The beans need to be soaked overnight two days before. The basic bean and vegetable soup is made just the day before, then reheated and ladled over toasted garlic bread, sprinkled with olive oil and served with lots of Parmesan cheese.

Put the beans in a bowl, cover with cold water, soak overnight, then drain just before you're ready to use them.

The next day, heat half the olive oil in a large, heavy stockpot and add the onion, carrot and celery. Cook gently for 10 minutes, stirring frequently. Add the leeks and garlic and cook for 10 minutes. Add the white cabbage, potato and courgettes, stir well and cook for 10 minutes, stirring frequently.

Stir in the soaked beans, passata, rosemary, thyme, sage, dried chilli, salt and plenty of black pepper. Cover with about 2 litres water (the vegetables should be well covered), bring to the boil, then turn down the heat and simmer, covered, for at least 2 hours, until the beans are very soft.

Take out 2–3 large ladles of soup and mash well. Stir back into the soup to thicken it. Stir in the cavolo nero or Savoy cabbage and simmer for another 15 minutes.

Remove from the heat, leave to cool, then refrigerate overnight. The next day, slowly reheat the soup and stir in the remaining olive oil. Toast the bread and rub with garlic. Pile the bread in a tureen or in individual bowls and ladle the soup over the top. Trickle in more olive oil and add plenty of grated Parmesan. To finish, stir in the Parmesan, then season to taste. Ladle into bowls and serve hot, warm or cold (but never chilled), with a little more Parmesan separately.

pasta & bean soup

pasta & *bean* soup

Italy produces the most wonderful, comforting soups and this one combines two of the great standbys – beans and pasta.

serves
6

M

Put the beans in a bowl, cover with cold water, add a pinch of bicarbonate of soda, soak overnight, then drain just before you're ready to use them.

The next day, put the drained beans in a large saucepan. Add the olive oil, garlic and stock. Bring to the boil, reduce the heat and simmer, part-covered with a lid, for 1–2 hours or until the beans are tender.

Working it batches if necessary, blend the beans with the cooking liquid using a blender or food processor. Return the bean purée to the rinsed-out pan, adding extra water or stock as necessary. Add the pasta and simmer gently for 15 minutes until tender. (Add a little extra water or stock if the soup is looking too thick.) Stir in the tomatoes and parsley and season well.

185 g dried cannellini or haricot beans

a pinch of bicarbonate of soda

4 tablespoons olive oil

2 garlic cloves, crushed

1.75 litres Chicken Stock (page 53)

100 g short pasta shapes, such as maccheroni or tubetti

4 tomatoes, skinned, deseeded and coarsely chopped

4 tablespoons freshly chopped flat leaf parsley

salt and black pepper

creamy *tomato* & *bread* soup

This is one of the most comforting soups on earth and has its origins in peasant thrift. Leftover bread is never thrown away in Tuscany – there is always a use for it. Here, it thickens a rich tomato soup, which is in turn enriched with Parmesan.

serves
6

V

Heat the oil in a large saucepan, add the onion and tomatoes and fry over gentle heat for about 10 minutes until soft. Push the mixture through a sieve and stir into the hot stock. Add the bread and garlic.

Cover and simmer gently for about 45 minutes until thick and creamy, whisking from time to time to break up the bread. Take care, because this soup can catch on the bottom.

To finish, stir the Parmesan into the soup, then season to taste. Serve hot, warm or cold (but never chilled), with a little more Parmesan separately.

4 tablespoons olive oil

1 onion, chopped

1.25 kg very ripe, soft tomatoes, coarsely chopped

1.5 litres hot Vegetable Stock (page 54)

300 g stale white bread, thinly sliced, crusts removed (or breadcrumbs)

3 garlic cloves, crushed

125 g grated Parmesan, plus extra to serve

salt and black pepper

stovetop wonders & stews

sausages with winter *rösti*

Potato rösti with a difference – celeriac. There is no doubting that celeriac is a gnarly, unattractive vegetable but get over that and you will be richly rewarded. Like celery, but sweeter, it gives a base note that enhances the flavour of the other ingredients it is cooked with. The rösti are perfect paired with some tasty sausages.

serves
4

M

8 pork sausages

2 tablespoons olive oil

Dijon mustard, to serve

Celeriac rösti

3 potatoes, unpeeled and halved

1 small head of celeriac (about 800 g), peeled and quartered

3 tablespoons unsalted butter

3 tablespoons olive oil

salt and black pepper

Put the potatoes and celeriac in a saucepan and cover with cold water. Bring to the boil, then immediately remove from the heat and cover with a lid. Set aside for 10 minutes. Drain well and leave to cool completely.

Grate the potatoes and celeriac into a bowl with 1 teaspoon salt and some black pepper. Toss to combine. Heat half the butter and 1 tablespoon of the oil in a large non-stick frying pan over high heat, swirling the butter around to coat the bottom of the pan. Add the potato mixture and gently press down to form a large cake. Cook for 5 minutes over high heat. Pour 1 tablespoon of olive oil around the very edge of the pan and gently shake the pan often to prevent the rösti from sticking to the bottom. Reduce the heat to medium and cook for 10 minutes, shaking the pan often.

Take a plate slightly larger than the pan. Place it on top of the pan then carefully invert the rösti onto the plate. Add the remaining oil and butter to the pan, then carefully slide the rösti back into the pan, cooked side up, and cook for 10 minutes.

Meanwhile, to cook the sausages, heat the oil in a frying pan over medium heat. Prick the sausages with a fork, add them to the pan and cook for about 20 minutes, turning often, to cook an even golden brown. Spoon the rösti directly from the pan onto serving plates and serve with the sausages and a little mustard on the side.

braised *pork* chops with *tomatoes*

serves
4–6

M

Braising is a fantastic way to cook thick pork chops, because it makes the meat so tender. This dish is very homely and perfect with potatoes, preferably fried or mashed.

3 tablespoons olive oil

8 bone-in pork chops, trimmed

3 celery sticks, chopped

1 onion, chopped

4 garlic cloves, chopped

½–1 teaspoon chilli flakes

125 ml red wine

400 g tinned chopped tomatoes

juice of 1 orange (and reserve the orange)

1 dried bay leaf

a few sprigs of fresh oregano or thyme

salt

Heat 2 tablespoons of the oil in a large sauté pan with a lid. Add the pork and cook until browned, 3–5 minutes. Turn and cook the other side. Transfer to a plate, season with salt and set aside.

Add the celery and onion and cook over high heat until browned, about 2–3 minutes. Add the garlic and chilli flakes and cook for 30 seconds. Add the wine and stir, scraping any bits that stick to the bottom of the pan. Boil for 1 minute, then stir in the tomatoes, orange juice, bay leaf, oregano and salt to taste. Quarter the reserved orange and put 1 piece in the sauce.

Return the meat to the pan and bury it under the sauce as much as possible. Cover, lower the heat and simmer gently until tender, about 1 hour. Turn the meat halfway through cooking.

Remove the meat from the sauce. Raise the heat under the tomato sauce and cook for 3–5 minutes to thicken slightly. Remove and discard the orange piece, bay leaf and herbs before serving.

fried *meatballs*

makes
15

Q

M

These meatballs are a Greek recipe and made lighter than other meatballs with the addition of soaked bread. Serve with rice.

3 slices of bread (crusts discarded), soaked in water

500 g minced beef or lamb

1 tablespoon lemon juice or white wine

1 onion, grated

1 egg, lightly beaten

1 tablespoon dried oregano

a handful of mint, chopped

5 tablespoons plain flour

4–5 tablespoons sunflower oil

salt and black pepper

Drain the bread and squeeze out the excess water, then put the bread in a bowl. Add the beef or lamb, lemon juice, onion, egg, oregano, mint, salt and pepper. Mix it with your fingers until well amalgamated.

Put the flour on a work surface. Make round, walnut-sized balls of the mince mixture, then roll them lightly in the flour. If you prefer, you can make them bigger, then flatten them – this will make frying quicker.

Heat the oil in a non-stick frying pan, add the meatballs and fry, turning them around until golden on all sides and cooked through. Remove and drain on kitchen paper, then serve immediately.

*braised pork chops
with tomatoes*

sage pork chops with *kale* colcannon

Easy to prepare, these sage-crumbed pork chops are served here with Irish-style colcannon. This is comfort food at its best – a creamy mashed potato with cooked cabbage. This colcannon recipe uses kale, a close relative of the cabbage. This is a true cold weather vegetable that actually relies on frost to enhance its flavour. So as the weather gets colder, the kale gets better, making it the perfect choice for late autumn.

serves
4

M

Put the plain flour on a flat plate. Mix the eggs and Worcestershire sauce in a bowl and, in a separate bowl, combine the sage, breadcrumbs and Parmesan. Press a pork chop into the flour, coating the meat evenly, then dip it in the egg mixture, then press firmly to coat in the crumb mix. Repeat this process with all 4 pork chops. Transfer them to a plate and refrigerate until needed.

To make the colcannon, cook the kale in a large saucepan of boiling water for 5 minutes. Drain well, chop finely and set aside.

Put 2 tablespoons of the butter in a frying pan over medium heat. Add the bacon and cook for 5 minutes, stirring occasionally until the bacon turns golden. Add the spring onions and cook for a further 2 minutes. Stir in the kale and remove the pan from the heat.

Put the potatoes in a large saucepan and cover with cold water. Bring to the boil and cook for 20 minutes, until soft when pierced with a skewer but not breaking apart. Drain the potatoes well and return them to the pan. Add the remaining butter and mash well. Beat with a wooden spoon until smooth. Stir the kale mixture into the potatoes, cover and keep warm while cooking the pork.

Heat the vegetable oil in a large frying pan over medium heat. When hot, add the pork chops and cook for 6–7 minutes, so they gently sizzle in the oil and a golden crust forms. Turn over the pork chops and cook for 5 minutes on the other side. Serve with a generous portion of the kale colcannon.

60 g plain flour

3 eggs

2 tablespoons Worcestershire sauce

4–6 sage leaves, freshly chopped

100 g breadcrumbs

100 g Parmesan, grated

4 pork chops

60 ml vegetable oil

Kale colcannon

500 g curly kale

150 g unsalted butter, cubed

2 rashers of bacon, thinly sliced

6–8 spring onions, thinly sliced

4 large potatoes, quartered

frazzled *eggs & smoked gammon*

2 tablespoons wholegrain mustard

1 tablespoon clear honey

4 smoked gammon steaks

2 tablespoons olive oil

4 large eggs

salt and black pepper

 serves 4

Q

M

The eggs here are fried quickly in very hot oil, giving them an almost lacy look and lovely crisp texture. This has to be one of the quickest and easiest dinners imaginable, with echoes of a wicked fried breakfast.

Preheat the grill.

Mix the mustard and honey together and brush over the gammon steaks. Grill for 2–3 minutes on each side, until cooked through. Cover loosely with foil and keep them warm while cooking the eggs.

Heat the oil in a frying pan until really hot. Add the eggs, 2 at a time, and cook until the whites are bubbly and crispy looking. Put an egg on top of each gammon steak. Sprinkle with salt and pepper and serve.

fresh fried *trout*

3 tablespoons olive oil

150 g bacon lardons or cubed ham

2 trout, cleaned

2 tablespoons plain flour, seasoned with salt and pepper

1 garlic clove, cut into slivers

2 tablespoons freshly chopped flat leaf parsley

salt and black pepper

1 lemon, cut into wedges, to serve

 serves 2

 Q

 M

F

You might feel that having a whole fish for dinner is not the route to thriftiness, but trout can be very inexpensive and this Spanish-inspired recipe uses few ingredients to excellent effect. You can eat it either hot or cold.

Heat 1 tablespoon of the oil in a frying pan, add the bacon and fry until just golden. Remove to a plate.

Dust the fish with the seasoned flour. Open the bellies, season with salt and pepper and put in the garlic slivers.

Heat the remaining oil in the frying pan, add the trout and fry for 3 minutes on each side. Increase the heat and cook for a further 2 minutes on each side. Transfer to hot plates, then return the bacon to the pan to warm through. Spoon the bacon on top of the trout and sprinkle with parsley and pepper. Serve hot with lemon wedges, or leave until cold.

*frazzled eggs &
smoked gammon*

easy tuna fish cakes

easy *tuna* fish cakes

Cornmeal makes a lovely crumb coating on these fish cakes, which are incredibly easy to make. Children love them too, so it's a good way to get them to eat fish.

Cook the sweet potatoes in a pan of simmering water for 20 minutes. Drain well and mash. Add the tuna, spring onions and egg, season and mix well. Divide the mixture into 8 equal pieces and shape into patties.

Put the cornmeal on a plate and dip the fish cakes in it until coated on all sides. Heat the oil and fry the fish cakes on each side until golden. Serve with lemon wedges and a tomato salad.

serves
4

F

600 g sweet potatoes, chopped

300 g tinned tuna, flaked

2 spring onions, chopped

1 egg

100 g cornmeal or polenta

3 tablespoons olive oil

salt and black pepper

1 lemon, to serve

tomato salad, to serve (optional)

Thai *salmon* fish cakes

Serve these delicious, aromatic fish cakes with their dipping sauce and stir-fried green vegetables, salad or noodles.

Put the spring onions, chilli flakes, coriander, lime leaves, lemongrass and eggs in a food processor and blend until finely chopped. Pick any bones out of the tinned salmon and discard. Add the salmon to the food processor, season and process briefly until the ingredients are combined; the mixture will be quite loose, but the cakes will hold together when cooked.

Heat 2 tablespoons oil in a large non-stick frying pan. Put 2 tablespoons of the mixture per fish cake in the pan – you will probably be able to cook 3–4 at a time. Fry the fish cakes for about 3 minutes until the bottom is set and golden, then carefully turn them over and cook for another 2–3 minutes.

Drain the fish cakes on kitchen paper and keep warm. Repeat to make about 12.

Meanwhile, mix together the ingredients for the dipping sauce in a bowl. Serve the fish cakes with a small bowl of the dipping sauce.

serves
4

Q

F

4 spring onions, sliced

½ teaspoon dried chilli flakes

2 tablespoons freshly chopped coriander

2 kaffir lime leaves, sliced

2 teaspoons finely chopped lemongrass

2 eggs

400 g tinned salmon, drained

salt and black pepper

sunflower oil, for frying

Dipping sauce

8 cm cucumber, deseeded and diced

2.5 cm fresh ginger, peeled and finely chopped

½ teaspoon light brown soft sugar

1 tablespoon Thai fish sauce

juice of ½ lime

1 tablespoon soy sauce

naked *spinach* & *ricotta* ravioli with *sage* cream

1 kg spinach, chopped

250 g ricotta

5 egg yolks

125 g Parmesan, finely grated, plus extra to serve

125 g plain flour

1 tablespoon unsalted butter

12 fresh sage leaves

250 ml single cream

salt and black pepper

a baking tray, lined with greaseproof paper

These little balls of spinach and ricotta are called 'naked' ravioli, as they are missing the pasta wrapping that usually encloses the filling. They look rather smart but they are in fact a good option for anyone on a budget, as they require just a few simple ingredients. They can be made a day in advance and chilled in the fridge until you are ready to cook them.

Bring a large saucepan of water to the boil. Add the spinach and cook for 5 minutes, until wilted and tender. Rinse with cold water and drain well.

Tip the cooked spinach into the centre of a clean tea towel. (This process will stain the tea towel so use an old, threadbare one, rather than your best.) Roll the tea towel up to form a log and twist the ends away from each other to squeeze out as much liquid as possible. Put the spinach on a chopping board and chop finely. Transfer to a large bowl. Add the ricotta, egg yolks and half the Parmesan and season to taste. Mix well to thoroughly combine.

Put the flour on a large plate. Using slightly wet hands, roll the spinach mixture into 12 walnut-sized balls. Lightly roll each ball in the flour and put them on the prepared baking tray.

Put the butter and sage in a small saucepan and set over medium heat. Cook until the sage leaves just sizzle. Add the cream and the remaining Parmesan and cook for about 10 minutes, until thickened, stirring often to prevent the cream from catching on the bottom of the pan.

Bring a large saucepan of lightly salted water to the boil. Carefully drop the balls into the boiling water and cook for just 1 minute, until they rise to the surface. Drain well and arrange 4 balls in each serving dish. Spoon over the warm sage cream, sprinkle with the extra Parmesan and grind over plenty of black pepper. Serve immediately.

pepperoni, red pepper & crouton frittata

4 eggs, beaten

25 g Gruyère cheese, grated

1 spring onion, thinly sliced

25 g unsalted butter

50 g firm white bread, torn into small pieces

1 garlic clove, crushed

25 g chargrilled red peppers, cut into strips

25 g pepperoni, sliced

salt and black pepper

a medium-sized, ovenproof frying pan

serves 2

Q

M

A frittata is Italy's version of an open omelette and it wins hands down as one of the most convenient ways to use up leftover bits and bobs in the fridge. This one is packed with tasty chargrilled peppers and pepperoni, and must be served immediately, otherwise it goes on cooking and loses its soft creaminess. It can also be left to cool, cut into wedges and enjoyed as part of a lunch-on-the-go the following day.

Break the eggs into a bowl and beat well using a fork. Season well and add half the cheese and spring onion. Mix well.

Melt half the butter in the ovenproof frying pan. Add the bread pieces and toss them for 2–3 minutes over high heat until golden brown and crispy. Remove from the heat and set aside.

Preheat the grill.

Add the remaining butter and the garlic to the pan, and when the butter starts to froth, add the beaten eggs. Turn the heat down and leave the eggs to cook gently for a few minutes. Arrange the pepperoni and chargrilled peppers on the top and sprinkle with the remaining cheese and reserved croutons. Put the frying pan under the preheated grill and cook for a further 2–3 minutes until the frittata is puffed and just set but still wobbly. Remove from the grill and serve immediately with a crisp green salad or a tomato and basil salad.

Variation: Also delicious made with any combination of the following: crumbled firm goats' cheese, sliced mushrooms, baby spinach leaves, courgettes or sliced cooked potatoes.

sausage, potato & onion tortilla

Loaded with sausages, fried potatoes and onions, this dish is perfect comfort food. Ring the changes with different kinds of sausage – try slices of chorizo, Italian sausages or frankfurters.

serves 2–3

M

3–4 tablespoons olive or sunflower oil

6 pork chipolata sausages

3 potatoes, about 325 g, thinly sliced

1 onion, halved then slivered lengthways

5 large eggs, beaten and seasoned with salt and pepper

salt and black pepper

a 20-cm heavy non-stick frying pan

Heat 1 tablespoon of the oil in the frying pan. Add the sausages and fry for 8–10 minutes, turning them frequently. Remove and set aside. Wipe the pan with kitchen paper, then heat another 2 tablespoons of the oil. Add the potatoes, layering them with the onion. Cook for 10–15 minutes over medium-low heat, lifting and turning occasionally, until just tender. The potatoes and onion should not brown very much.

Put the beaten eggs in a bowl. Remove the potatoes and onions from the pan with a slotted spoon and add to the eggs. Thickly slice the sausages and mix with the eggs and potatoes.

Return the frying pan to the heat, adding a little more oil if necessary. Add the egg mixture, spreading it evenly. Cook over medium-low heat until the bottom is golden brown and the top has almost set. Put a plate on top of the pan and invert the pan. Slide the tortilla back into the pan, brown side up, and cook for 2–3 minutes until lightly browned underneath.

pepperoni, red pepper & crouton frittata

sausage, potato & onion tortilla

3 tablespoons olive oil

1 onion, chopped

1 garlic clove, crushed

3 ripe plum tomatoes, chopped

1 red chilli, deseeded and finely chopped

2 tablespoons tomato purée

150 ml white wine or water

325 g cold cooked spaghetti (140 g before cooking)

6 large eggs, beaten

2 tablespoons grated Parmesan

25 g rocket

2 tablespoons balsamic vinegar

salt and black pepper

a 24-cm heavy ovenproof frying pan

spaghetti & *rocket* frittata

serves 4

V

This is great for using up leftover spaghetti. It's mixed with a fiery tomato and chilli sauce.

Heat 1 tablespoon of the oil in a saucepan, add the onion and sauté for 5 minutes until softened. Add the garlic, tomatoes and chilli and cook for 3–4 minutes, stirring several times. Add the tomato purée and wine or water and simmer for 5 minutes. Remove from the heat, add the spaghetti and toss gently.

Put the eggs in a bowl. Add the spaghetti and sauce and mix gently. Heat the remaining oil in the frying pan, add the spaghetti and egg mixture and cook over low heat for 10–12 minutes, or until golden brown on the underside and almost set on the top.

Preheat the grill.

Sprinkle with the Parmesan and slide under the grill for 30–60 seconds to melt the cheese and finish cooking the top. Leave to cool for 5 minutes, then transfer to a plate. Put the rocket on top of the frittata, sprinkle with balsamic vinegar and serve.

6 large eggs, beaten

8 sun-dried tomatoes in oil, drained and sliced

1 tablespoon freshly chopped sage leaves

50 g pitted black olives, thickly sliced

50 g Parmesan, grated

2 tablespoons olive oil

1 onion, halved and sliced

salt and black pepper

a 20-cm ovenproof frying pan

sun-dried tomato frittata

serves 2–3

Q

V

If you have the time, it is worth mixing the tomatoes and sage into the eggs an hour before cooking for a more intense flavour.

Put the eggs, sun-dried tomatoes, sage, olives, Parmesan and some seasoning in a bowl and mix gently.

Heat the oil in the frying pan, add the onion and cook over low heat until soft and golden. Increase the heat to medium, pour the egg mixture into the pan and stir just long enough to mix in the onion. Cook over medium-low heat until the base of the frittata is golden and the top has almost set.

Preheat the grill.

Slide the pan under the grill to finish cooking or put a plate on top of the pan and invert the pan. Slide the tortilla back into the pan, brown side up, and cook for 1–2 minutes until lightly browned underneath.

field mushroom tortilla

field mushroom tortilla

Use up some leftover boiled potatoes in this simple tortilla.

serves
4–6

Q

V

Heat the butter and olive oil in the frying pan, add the potatoes and brown on all sides. Transfer to a plate, then cook the mushrooms on both sides for 5 minutes, adding a little more oil or butter if necessary. Transfer to another plate and return the potatoes to the pan. Sprinkle in the garlic, then add the mushrooms and spinach.

Mix the eggs and milk together, season and pour into the pan. Cover and cook gently for 5 minutes.

Preheat the grill to medium-high.

Put the tortilla under the grill for 6–8 minutes, or until golden on top.

20 g unsalted butter

2 tablespoons olive oil

3 cooked potatoes, diced

200 g flat field mushrooms

1 garlic clove, crushed

125 g baby spinach

4 eggs

100 ml milk

salt and black pepper

a medium-sized, ovenproof frying pan

classic Spanish tortilla

classic Spanish tortilla

This is the classic tortilla consisting of just three ingredients – eggs, potatoes and onions – making an incredibly delicious dish.

Cut the onion in half, then slice thinly lengthways and separate into slivers. Heat 3 tablespoons of the oil in the frying pan.

Add the potatoes to the pan in layers, alternating with the onion. Cook for 10–15 minutes over medium-low heat, turning occasionally, until just tender. Remove the potatoes and onions from the pan and drain in a colander, reserving any oil. Put the eggs and vegetables in a bowl and mix gently.

Heat the reserved oil in the pan, adding a little extra if necessary. Add the potato and egg mixture, spreading it evenly in the pan. Cook over medium-low heat until the bottom is golden brown and the top almost set.

Put a plate on top of the frying pan and invert the pan. Slide the tortilla back into the pan, brown side up, and cook for 2–3 minutes until lightly browned underneath.

1 large onion

3–4 tablespoons olive or sunflower oil

4 potatoes, about 500 g, thinly sliced

5 large eggs, beaten and seasoned with salt and pepper

salt and black pepper

a 20-cm heavy non-stick frying pan

chickpea tortilla

Chickpeas are a delicious alternative to potato in a Spanish tortilla, adding a slightly sweet, nutty flavour.

Break the eggs into a large bowl, add salt, pepper and paprika and whisk briefly with a fork. Stir in the chopped parsley.

Heat 2 tablespoons of the oil in the frying pan. Add the onion and red pepper and cook for about 5 minutes until softened, turning frequently. Add the garlic and chickpeas and cook for 2 minutes. Transfer to the bowl of eggs and stir gently. Add the remaining oil to the pan and return to the heat. Add the chickpea mixture, spreading it evenly in the pan. Cook over medium-low heat until the bottom is golden brown and the top almost set.

Put a plate on top of the frying pan and invert the pan. Slide the tortilla back into the pan, brown side up, and cook for 2–3 minutes until lightly browned underneath.

5 large eggs

½ teaspoon Spanish smoked paprika

3 tablespoons freshly chopped flat leaf parsley

3 tablespoons olive oil

1 large onion, finely chopped

1 red pepper, halved, deseeded and chopped

2 garlic cloves, finely chopped

400 g tinned chickpeas, rinsed and well drained

salt and black pepper

a 20-cm heavy non-stick frying pan

smoky *sausage* & *bean* casserole

serves
4

M

1 tablespoon light olive oil

12 chipolata sausages

1 garlic clove, chopped

1 leek, thinly sliced

1 carrot, diced

1 celery stick, diced

400 g tinned chopped
tomatoes

1 teaspoon Spanish smoked
paprika

2 tablespoons maple syrup

2 sprigs of fresh thyme

400 g tinned cannellini beans,
drained and rinsed

The Italians use a mixture of onions, carrots and celery sautéed in olive oil as the base for many soups and casseroles and it's right at home here in a hearty stew with sausages and beans.

Heat the oil in a heavy-based casserole or saucepan over high heat. Add the sausages in two batches and cook them for 4–5 minutes, turning often until cooked and an even brown all over. Remove from the casserole.

Add the garlic, leek, carrot and celery and cook for 5 minutes, stirring often. Add the tomatoes, paprika, maple syrup, thyme, beans and 500 ml water and return the sausages to the pan. Bring to the boil, then reduce the heat to medium and simmer for 40–45 minutes, until the sauce has thickened.

Tip: Replace the sausages with 500 g pork neck fillet cut into 2–3-cm pieces. Cook the pork in batches for 4–5 minutes each batch, turning often so each piece is evenly browned. Return all the pork to the pan, as you would the sausages, and simmer for 45–50 minutes until the pork is tender.

chicken with *tomatoes* & *olives*

serves
4–6

M

2 tablespoons olive oil

1 chicken, about 2 kg,
cut into 6–8 pieces

8 garlic cloves, finely
chopped

400 g tinned chopped
tomatoes

a pinch of sugar

50 g black olives,
pitted and chopped

salt and black pepper

a bunch of fresh basil, torn

Versions of this basic but flavoursome chicken dish are eaten in homes all over France. This one from the south-east is particularly appealing and goes well with rice or fresh pasta.

Heat 1 tablespoon of the olive oil in a large saucepan. Add the chicken pieces and brown on all sides. Transfer the chicken to a plate, salt generously and set aside. Add the remaining oil and garlic and cook for 1 minute; do not let it burn. Add the tomatoes and sugar. Stir well and return the chicken pieces to the pan. Cover and simmer gently until the chicken is cooked through, about 25–30 minutes.

Transfer the chicken pieces to a serving dish, then raise the heat and cook the sauce to thicken slightly, about 10 minutes. Season to taste, then stir in the olives. Pour the sauce over the chicken pieces, sprinkle with the basil and serve immediately.

*smoky sausage &
bean casserole*

beef braised in *rooibos tea* with *sweet potatoes*

Rooibos (or Redbush) is a rich, lightly honey-flavoured tea which doesn't have any bitter tannins. It is said to have tenderizing qualities too, so it works particularly well in this stew recipe. Brisket of beef is a good, thrifty cut which is ideal for pot-roasting and results in a meltingly tender texture.

Season the brisket and coat in the flour. Heat the vegetable oil in a casserole dish, then add the brisket and cook over medium heat for a few minutes until golden brown all over.

Add the onions and celery and stir, then cover with a tight-fitting lid and leave to soften for 10 minutes. Add the garlic and tomato purée and cook for 1 minute.

Meanwhile, brew the tea. Put the tea bags in a large heatproof jug and pour over 1 litre boiling hot water. Leave to steep for 4 minutes, then strain into the casserole, along with the vinegar, orange zest, cinnamon and ginger. Turn the heat to low, cover with the lid and cook for 2 hours, or until the meat has become quite tender. Add the sweet potatoes, honey and plenty of seasoning and cook for a further 30 minutes, or until the potatoes are tender. Garnish with the coriander, if using, and serve.

600 g brisket or stewing beef, trimmed of some fat and cut into 5-cm pieces

2 tablespoons plain flour

1 tablespoon vegetable oil

2 onions, sliced

2 celery sticks, sliced

3 garlic cloves, crushed

1 tablespoon tomato purée

5 Rooibos tea bags

5 tablespoons red wine vinegar

4 strips of orange zest

2 cinnamon sticks

4 cm fresh ginger, peeled and thickly sliced

4 small sweet potatoes, thickly sliced

150 g clear honey

salt and black pepper

a handful of fresh coriander leaves, to garnish (optional)

1 tablespoon olive oil

2 garlic cloves, crushed

1 onion, diced

2 celery sticks, diced

800 g chuck steak, cubed

400 ml hot Beef Stock (page 53)

200 ml red wine

2 dried bay leaves

4 carrots, chopped

25 g plain flour

salt and black pepper

Dumplings

200 g plain flour

75 g hard vegetable fat

1 teaspoon baking powder

75 g strong Cheddar, grated

1 medium chicken

2 celery sticks, chopped

1 red onion, chopped

2 garlic cloves, finely sliced

3 carrots, chopped

1 turnip, about 200 g, chopped

2 dried bay leaves

1 sprig of fresh rosemary

2 sprigs of fresh thyme

8 small waxy potatoes

½ Savoy cabbage

salt and black pepper

beef & carrot casserole with cheesy dumplings

serves 4–6

M

The feather-light dumplings nestling in the rich, savoury casserole will have everyone demanding more.

Heat the oil in a large casserole dish, add the garlic, onion and celery and sauté for 4 minutes. Transfer to a plate. Put the beef in the casserole, increase the heat and sauté for 5 minutes, stirring frequently. When the beef is cooked, return the onion mixture to the casserole. Add the stock, red wine, seasoning and bay leaves, bring to the boil, then reduce the heat to a gentle simmer. Cover and cook for 1½ hours.

To make the dumplings, put the flour and baking powder in a bowl and rub in the fat until it resembles breadcrumbs. Add the cheese, mixing it in with a knife. Add 75–100 ml water and use your hands to bring the mixture together and form a dough. Divide into 8 equal pieces and roll into balls.

Remove the casserole from the heat for 5 minutes. Sift in the flour and stir to thicken. Return to the heat and add the carrots. Stir until the casserole comes to a simmer. Place the dumplings on top, cover and cook for 20 minutes.

chicken in a pot

serves 4–6

M

This is hearty, good-value family fare – a whole chicken plus herbs and vegetables, all in the same pot for minimum effort.

Cut any excess fat or skin off the chicken and place the bird in a large casserole dish. Add the celery, onion, garlic, carrots, turnip, herbs and seasoning. Add just enough water to cover, then place on the heat and bring to the boil. Reduce to a simmer, then cover and cook for 45 minutes. Add the potatoes and cook for a further 25 minutes. Spoon off any excess fat floating on the top of the casserole. Trim the cabbage and cut into 4 wedges, add to the pot, cover and cook for 4 minutes.

Remove the chicken, cut into joints and serve, ladling over the vegetables and stock at the table.

beef & carrot
casserole with
cheesy dumplings

coq au leftover *red wine*

Any leftover red wine will do for this recipe – if you have genuine leftovers that are no longer drinkable, it's better to put them to good use than to waste them. Consider using chicken drumsticks in recipes that typically call for a whole bird to be cut into portions. It saves you some chopping and you can more easily calculate portion size and keep the cost down – allow two drumsticks per person. The chicken marinates in the wine overnight, so you'll need to start prepping the day before you intend to serve. The perfect accompaniment is garlic mash.

serves 4

M

Put the chicken drumsticks in a non-reactive dish with the red wine, onion, carrot, celery, garlic and bay leaf. Cover and refrigerate overnight, turning occasionally. Set a colander over a large bowl and tip the entire contents of the dish into it. Remove the chicken drumsticks and leave the vegetables in the colander to drain. Reserve the marinating liquid.

Heat 1 tablespoon of the oil in a casserole dish or large, heavy-based saucepan and cook the pickling onions and bacon for 4–5 minutes, shaking the pan often, until golden. Remove from the pan and set aside. Add another tablespoon of the oil to the pan and cook the mushrooms for 5 minutes, until golden and softened. Remove from the pan and set aside.

Add another tablespoon of the oil to the pan and cook half the chicken drumsticks for a few minutes until well browned all over. Transfer to a plate. Add the remaining oil and drumsticks to the pan and repeat. Add the drained vegetables, garlic and bay leaf to the pan and cook for 5 minutes, until softened and golden.

Return the chicken, pickling onions and bacon to the pan along with the reserved marinating liquid and the beef stock. Bring to the boil, then reduce the heat to medium, cover and cook for about 20 minutes, until the chicken is cooked through and tender. Add the mushrooms and cook for 5 minutes.

Meanwhile, to make the garlic mash, cook the potatoes in a large saucepan of lightly salted boiling water for 15 minutes, until very tender. Drain well and return to the warm pan. Put the milk, garlic and butter in a small saucepan and cook over low heat until melted. Add the milk mixture to the potatoes and mash or beat until smooth and fluffy. Season to taste. Serve with the chicken casserole.

8 chicken drumsticks

250 ml red wine

1 onion, chopped

1 carrot, diced

1 celery stick, diced

4 garlic cloves, sliced

1 dried bay leaf

4 tablespoons olive oil

12 pickling onions or small shallots

4 rashers of bacon, chopped

100 g button mushrooms, stalks removed

500 ml beef stock

salt and black pepper

Garlic mash

800 g floury potatoes, quartered or halved, depending on size

125 ml milk

3 garlic cloves, crushed

75 g unsalted butter

spicy *pork* curry with *lemon* rice

2 tomatoes, chopped

2 large green chillies, chopped

4 garlic cloves

1 onion, chopped

2 teaspoons ground cumin

5 cm fresh ginger, grated

a small bunch of fresh coriander, roots and stalks roughly chopped and leaves reserved to garnish

2 tablespoons vegetable oil

750 g pork shoulder, cut into bite-sized pieces

2 tablespoons white vinegar

very finely shredded fresh ginger, to garnish

Lemon rice

400 g basmati rice

½ teaspoon turmeric

3 tablespoons unsalted butter

4–6 dried curry leaves

½ teaspoon brown mustard seeds

2 teaspoons finely grated lemon zest

1 tablespoon lemon juice

serves
4

M

It's useful to have a curry recipe to hand that does not require a vast number of different spices. With the exception of the ground cumin, the curry paste that forms the basis of this recipe calls for fresh ingredients. If pork is not your thing, simply replace it with the same quantity of a stewing steak like chuck – the cooking time will be the same.

Put the tomatoes, chillies, garlic, onion, cumin, ginger, coriander roots and stalks and oil in a food processor and process until smooth. Put the paste in a casserole dish or heavy-based saucepan and cook for 5 minutes, stirring constantly, until golden and aromatic.

Put the pork in the casserole, add 1 litre water and bring to the boil, stirring occasionally. Reduce the heat to low so that the liquid just gently simmers and cook, uncovered, for 1½ hours, stirring often so that the meat doesn't catch and burn. Stir in the vinegar.

Meanwhile, to make the lemon rice, rinse the rice in several changes of cold water. Bring a large saucepan of water to the boil and add the turmeric. Add the rice and cook for 10–12 minutes, until tender. Drain well and return to the warm pan. Heat the butter in a small saucepan set over high heat and cook the curry leaves and mustard seeds until they start to sizzle. Add to the rice along with the lemon zest and juice and stir well to combine. Garnish the curry with shredded ginger and the coriander leaves and serve with the lemon rice.

kofta curry

serves
4

These 'kofta', or meatballs, are cooked in a spicy tomato sauce. Serve them with warm naan bread or steamed basmati rice.

To make the koftas, put the ginger, garlic, cinnamon, coriander and lamb, beef or pork in a mixing bowl. Season well and, using your fingers, mix well to combine. Roll tablespoons of the mixture into bite-sized balls, place on a tray, cover and chill for 1–2 hours.

Heat 2 tablespoons of the sunflower oil in a large, non-stick frying pan, then add the koftas and cook in batches until lightly browned. Remove with a slotted spoon and set aside.

Add the remaining oil to the pan and place over medium heat. Add the onion and stir-fry for 4–5 minutes, then stir in the curry paste. Stir-fry for 1–2 minutes, then add the tinned tomatoes and stock. Bring to the boil, reduce the heat to low and simmer gently, uncovered, for 10–15 minutes.

Add the koftas to the pan and stir carefully to coat them in the sauce. Simmer gently for 10–15 minutes, or until cooked through. Stir in the cream and cook for a final 2–3 minutes. Remove from the heat and garnish with the extra coriander leaves.

3 tablespoons sunflower oil

1 onion, finely chopped

2 tablespoons medium curry paste

400 g tinned chopped tomatoes

200 ml hot Chicken Stock (page 53)

150 ml double cream

Koftas

2 teaspoons finely grated fresh ginger

4 teaspoons crushed garlic

1 teaspoon ground cinnamon

8 tablespoons freshly chopped coriander leaves, plus extra to garnish

800 g minced lamb, beef or pork

lamb kefta tagine

Moroccan cooking uses a relatively short list of staple spices, such as cumin, cinnamon and cayenne pepper, but they are used in varying quantities to produce very different results from one recipe to the next. A tagine is a Moroccan stew traditionally cooked in a large-lidded terracotta pot, which gives the dish its name, but you can use a large frying pan.

serves
4

M

500 g minced lamb

1 onion, grated

2 garlic cloves, finely chopped

a handful of fresh flat leaf parsley, finely chopped

2 tablespoons olive oil

1 teaspoon ground cumin

1 teaspoon ground cinnamon

½ teaspoon cayenne pepper

400 g tinned chopped tomatoes

a handful of freshly chopped coriander

Put the lamb, half the onion, half the garlic and the parsley in a bowl. Use your hands to combine the mixture. Set aside.

Heat the oil in a large heavy-based frying pan set over high heat and cook the remaining onion and garlic for 5 minutes, until softened and golden. Add the spices and cook, stirring constantly, for 1 minute, until aromatic. Add the tomatoes and 250 ml water and bring to the boil. Cook for about 5 minutes.

With slightly wet hands, roll the lamb mixture into walnut-sized balls and put them directly into the sauce mixture as you do so. Reduce the heat, cover and cook for about 15 minutes, until the lamb is cooked through. Stir in the coriander and serve.

ratatouille

curried *lentils & spinach*

Forget any lentil dishes you may not have enjoyed in the past. This is just so delicious: all the extra flavours bring the lentils to life.

serves
4

V

Heat the oil in a medium saucepan, add the onion and cook for 5 minutes. Add the garlic, garam masala, curry powder and cardamom, mix well, then cook for 3 minutes.

Add the brown lentils and 500 ml water, bring to the boil, then reduce the heat and simmer for 20 minutes, stirring frequently.

When the lentils are soft, add the tomatoes, spinach, lemon juice, salt and pepper. Stir well and serve hot or warm.

4 tablespoons olive oil

1 onion, diced

1 garlic clove, chopped

1 teaspoon garam masala

1 teaspoon medium curry powder

½ teaspoon crushed cardamom pods

250 g brown lentils

2 tomatoes, skinned and chopped

175 g spinach, chopped

juice of 1 lemon

salt and black pepper

ratatouille

One of those reliable recipes that just gets better as it matures, ratatouille can be served with many dishes, and also by itself with lots of crusty bread. Don't use green peppers – they are too bitter. You'll need a little white wine so here's your chance to use up that bottle that's been sitting out for a few days.

serves
6

V

Cut the aubergines into large, bite-sized pieces, put them in a colander, sprinkle well with salt and leave to drain for 1 hour.

Heat the olive oil in a casserole dish and fry the onions, crushed garlic and coriander seeds until soft and transparent, but not coloured. Add the wine and boil to reduce.

Meanwhile, rinse and drain the aubergines and dry on kitchen paper. Add the peppers and aubergines to the casserole and cook for about 10 minutes, stirring occasionally until softening around the edges, but not browning. Add the tomatoes, sugar and olives. Heat to simmering point, season well, then half-cover and cook for about 25 minutes. Add the basil, if using, and serve hot or cold.

2 aubergines

3 tablespoons olive oil

2 large onions, thinly sliced

2 garlic cloves, crushed

2 teaspoons finely crushed coriander seeds

5 tablespoons white wine

3 peppers (red, yellow or orange), deseeded and cut into thick strips

400 g tinned chopped tomatoes

1 teaspoon sugar

about 20 pitted black olives

salt and black pepper

fresh basil leaves, to serve (optional)

pasta, rice & grains

*spaghetti &
meatballs*

spaghetti & meatballs

The milk-soaked bread and Parmesan keep these meatballs feather-light and impossibly moreish.

serves 4

M

Preheat the oven to 200°C (400°F) Gas 6.

Combine the pork, onion, egg, most of the garlic, parsley, Parmesan and salt and pepper. Put the bread in a small bowl and pour over the milk. Break the mixture up into small pieces then add to the bowl with the meat. Mix everything with your hands until well combined. Roll into 5-cm balls and place on a baking tray lined with aluminium foil. Bake in the preheated oven for 15 minutes, giving the meatballs a shake halfway through cooking so they don't stick. Set aside.

In a large saucepan, heat the olive oil and cook the remaining garlic until golden but not brown. Add the tomatoes and break up with a flat spoon. Season. Cook for 15 minutes, stirring every 5 minutes or so. Add the butter and the meatballs.

Cook the spaghetti until al dente. Drain and mix with the sauce. Serve sprinkled with grated Parmesan.

400 g minced pork or beef

1 small onion, finely chopped

1 egg, beaten

5 garlic cloves, crushed

3 tablespoons freshly chopped flat leaf parsley

3 tablespoons grated Parmesan, plus extra to serve

1 teaspoon each salt and ground black pepper

2 slices of white bread

3 tablespoons milk

5 tablespoons olive oil

3 x 400-g tins plum tomatoes

1 tablespoon unsalted butter

400 g spaghetti

spaghetti bolognese

Long, slow cooking is the secret of good bolognese sauce. It can be served with any shape of pasta, and a crisp green salad is the perfect accompaniment.

serves 4–6

M

Heat the oil in a large saucepan, add the garlic, onions, celery and carrot and sauté gently for 10 minutes. Add the beef, breaking it up with a wooden spoon, and cook for a further 10 minutes. Add the oregano, thyme, bay leaves, tomato purée and passata, season and mix well. Simmer for 1 hour, stirring frequently.

Cook the spaghetti according to the packet instructions. Drain well and divide between individual bowls. Stir the parsley into the sauce, then spoon onto the pasta and serve.

2 tablespoons olive oil

3 garlic cloves, crushed

2 onions, diced

1 celery stick, diced

1 carrot, diced

700 g minced beef

1 teaspoon dried oregano

a sprig of fresh thyme

2 dried bay leaves

2 tablespoons tomato purée

1 litre tomato passata

300 g spaghetti

a handful of fresh flat leaf parsley, chopped

salt and black pepper

grated Parmesan, to serve

400 g spaghetti, or similar pasta

90 ml olive oil

100 g breadcrumbs

8 small or baby courgettes, cut into julienne strips

2 garlic cloves, crushed

2 small red chillies, deseeded and chopped

grated Parmesan, to serve

spaghetti with chilli & courgettes

serves
4

Q

V

This is one of those pasta combinations that works with just about any of your favourite seasonings. You can easily use chilli flakes instead of fresh chillies.

Cook the spaghetti according to the packet instructions. Drain well and return to the pan to keep warm.

Meanwhile, heat a large frying pan over medium heat. Add half the olive oil, swirling around to coat the pan, then add the breadcrumbs. Cook for 3–4 minutes, stirring constantly until evenly browned with a nutty aroma. Remove from the pan and wipe the pan clean. Add the remaining oil to the pan and cook the courgettes for 5 minutes over high heat, turning often, until golden and starting to look crispy. Add the garlic and chillies and cook for 4–5 minutes, stirring often. Add the cooked pasta and breadcrumbs to the pan, tossing around to combine and serve immediately with grated Parmesan sprinkled over the top.

⅔ onion, finely chopped

250 ml hot Chicken Stock (page 53)

2 garlic cloves, crushed

1 red and 1 green pepper, deseeded and diced

2 teaspoons paprika

400 g tinned chopped tomatoes

1 tablespoon tomato purée

500 g wholemeal spaghetti

250 g green cabbage, chopped

salt and black pepper

Meatballs

½ onion, very finely chopped

500 g minced pork

2 tablespoons breadcrumbs

2 teaspoons paprika

1 teaspoon dried sage

goulash meatballs with pasta

serves
6

M

These meatballs are great for making in advance and can be frozen in individual portions.

Cook the onion in 4 tablespoons of the stock in a covered casserole dish for 4–5 minutes until softened. Stir in the garlic, peppers and paprika and cook for 1 minute, then add the tomatoes, tomato purée and the remaining stock. Season and simmer, uncovered, for 10 minutes.

While the sauce is cooking, mix the meatball ingredients together with seasoning and shape into 24 small balls. Brown the meatballs in 2 batches in a non-stick frying pan, then add to the sauce and simmer for 20 minutes.

Cook the spaghetti in a large saucepan of lightly salted boiling water for 7 minutes, then stir in the cabbage and cook for a further 5 minutes. Drain and divide the pasta and cabbage between bowls. Spoon the meatballs and sauce over the pasta and serve.

spaghetti with chilli & courgettes

puttanesca pasta sauce

puttanesca pasta sauce

The combination of ingredients in this classic sauce – olive oil, garlic, chillies, anchovies, tomatoes, olives and capers – packs a real punch and is probably to hand in your kitchen cupboards.

serves
4–6

F

olive oil, for cooking

1 garlic clove, finely chopped

1 small piece of dried chilli, finely chopped (to taste)

50 g tinned anchovy fillets, drained and mashed

800 g tinned chopped tomatoes, drained (reserve the juice)

50 g capers (if salted, rinse well and pat dry with kitchen paper)

100 g pitted black olives

500 g pasta, such as spaghetti or penne

black pepper

2 handfuls of fresh parsley, chopped

Cover the base of a medium saucepan with olive oil. Add the garlic and chilli and set over low heat. Remove the garlic clove as soon as it starts to turn golden. Add the mashed anchovy, chopped tomatoes, capers, olives and black pepper. Stir and continue cooking until the sauce has reduced and darkened in colour, about 20–30 minutes. If the sauce starts to dry out too much, stir in a little of the reserved tomato juice.

Cook the pasta according to the packet instructions. Drain well and add the sauce. Stir well, then transfer to a large serving dish, add the parsley and serve at once.

quick Neapolitan *tomato* sauce

This classic tomato sauce comes originally from Campania, the region around Naples. Make a large batch and freeze the bulk for a no-fuss supper another time.

serves
4–6

V

1 kg tinned chopped tomatoes, drained (reserve the juice)

5 tablespoons olive oil

4 garlic cloves

your choice of: 1 small piece of fresh chilli, ½ cinnamon stick, ½ teaspoon dried oregano, or a bunch of fresh herbs, chopped, such as basil

3 tablespoons grated Parmesan, plus extra to serve

500 g pasta

salt and black pepper

Put the tomatoes, oil and garlic in a heavy-based saucepan. Add your choice of the chilli, cinnamon and dried or fresh herbs. Cover and simmer over low heat for 30 minutes, or until the tomatoes have become creamy.

Stir from time to time to stop the sauce sticking to the bottom of the pan. Add a little of the reserved tomato juice whenever necessary to keep the sauce moist. Discard the garlic and chilli, cinnamon or herbs (if possible). Mash the sauce with a potato masher. Taste and adjust the seasoning.

Cook the pasta according to the packet instructions. Drain well, add the sauce and Parmesan and stir well. Transfer to a serving dish, then serve at once with extra Parmesan.

pesto

50 g fresh basil leaves

1 garlic clove, crushed

2 tablespoons pine nuts

a pinch of salt

6–8 tablespoons olive oil

2 tablespoons grated Parmesan

400 g pasta

black pepper

serves 4

Q

V

Over the past 20 years, this thick, aromatic herb and nut sauce from Genoa has travelled widely and is now used by cooks throughout the world to serve with pasta or grilled fish, or be stirred into vegetable soup. Once made, cover the surface with a little extra olive oil, seal in a container and refrigerate for up to 5 days.

Put the basil, garlic, pine nuts and salt in a mortar and pound to form a fairly smooth paste. Add the olive oil slowly until you reach a texture that is soft but not runny. Add the Parmesan and pepper to taste.

Cook the pasta according to the packet instructions. Drain well, add the pesto and stir through before serving.

Alternatively, cover the surface with a little olive oil and refrigerate for up to 3 days.

Tip: You can make this sauce in a food processor, but do not over-process otherwise the sauce will become too smooth.

tapenade

125 g niçoise olives

2 tinned anchovy fillets in oil, drained

2 garlic cloves, crushed

2 tablespoons capers in brine, drained and rinsed

1 teaspoon Dijon mustard

4 tablespoons olive oil

a squeeze of lemon juice

400 g pasta

black pepper

serves 4

Q

V

Using niçoise olives will give the finished sauce a truly authentic flavour. It is preferable to buy whole olives and pit them yourself – to do this simply press down firmly on the olives using a thumb and the flesh will split to reveal the stone, which is then discarded.

Put the olives, anchovies, garlic, capers and mustard in a mortar (or food processor) and pound to form a fairly smooth paste. Gradually blend in the olive oil and add lemon juice and pepper to taste.

Cook the pasta according to the packet instructions. Drain well, add the tapenade and stir through before serving.

Alternatively, transfer to a dish, cover and refrigerate for up to 5 days.

pot-luck summer *pasta*

Pasta is a great standby meal – quick to cook and always a favourite with kids. Its versatile nature means that you can throw just about anything from the storecupboard or the fridge in with it, whether it be vegetables, meat or fish. All you need to do then is add some home-made tomato sauce and/or béchamel, mix it and bake it in the oven.

Bring a 5-litre saucepan of water to the boil, add 2 teaspoons salt and the pasta and cook over high heat until slightly less than al dente. Drain, reserving 2 tablespoons of the cooking water, and return to the saucepan.

Meanwhile, cover the base of a medium saucepan with olive oil. Set over high heat, and when the oil is searing hot, add the tomatoes. Cook for 1–2 minutes, taking care not to burn the tomatoes, but allowing them to caramelize a little. Reduce the heat and mash the tomatoes with a potato masher, then add the garlic and oregano. Stir well, cover and cook for a few minutes, then add the mushrooms, if using, cover and cook for 20 minutes. Stir in the tuna, capers, peas and ham and heat through.

Preheat the oven to 220°C (425°F) Gas 7.

To make the béchamel sauce, melt the butter in a small saucepan, and when it starts to bubble, add the flour and mix well. Cook over gentle heat for 1–2 minutes, then whisk in the milk and continue cooking until the sauce thickens. Add grated nutmeg and salt to taste.

Add the sauce to the pasta with the reserved water and mix until the pasta is well coated. Stir in the mozzarella and salami, if using. Transfer to a large, shallow, greased baking dish and pour the béchamel sauce over the top. Sprinkle with the breadcrumbs. Drizzle with olive oil and bake in the preheated oven for 20–30 minutes, or until golden. Serve immediately.

serves 4
M
F

500 g penne or rigatoni

800 g tinned plum tomatoes, drained and deseeded

6 garlic cloves, crushed

1 teaspoon dried oregano or 1 small piece of chilli, to taste

150 g cooked peas, sweetcorn or sliced mushrooms

370 g tinned tuna in oil, half drained

100 g cooked ham or chicken, cut into slivers

1 tablespoon salted capers, rinsed, dried and chopped

150 g mozzarella cheese, diced

50 g salami, finely chopped (optional)

15 g breadcrumbs

olive oil, for frying and drizzling

salt

Béchamel sauce

40 g unsalted butter

40 g flour

400 ml warmed milk

freshly grated nutmeg

warm *pasta* salad with *tuna,* chilli & rocket

400 g large dried pasta shells, such as lumaconi

65 ml olive oil

2 red onions, finely chopped

2 garlic cloves, finely chopped

1 large red chilli, deseeded and finely chopped

2 tablespoons small salted capers, rinsed

1 tablespoon red wine vinegar

400 g tinned tuna in oil, well drained

50 g feta cheese, crumbled

50 g rocket

salt and black pepper

lemon wedges, to serve

serves
4

Q

F

Tinned fish is one of the most convenient and healthy fast foods to have on hand. It works so well with other simple, fresh Mediterranean flavours, such as lemon and parsley. The inclusion of feta cheese here may seem a little odd, but it really does work. Just a small amount provides an extra tangy, savoury element to this summery dish. Any large, open pasta shape will work, but lumaconi have been used in this particular recipe. 'Lumaconi' translates as 'big snail shells'.

Cook the pasta according to the packet instructions. Drain well and add 1 tablespoon of the olive oil. Transfer to a large bowl.

Heat the remaining oil in a large frying pan set over high heat. Add the onions, garlic, chilli and capers and cook, stirring, for 2–3 minutes, until the onion has softened. Add the vinegar and cook for a further minute. Add the tuna and use a fork to roughly break up any larger chunks, without mushing the tuna too much.

Add the tuna mixture to the bowl with the pasta. Add the feta and rocket and gently toss to combine. Season to taste with salt and a generous amount of pepper. Serve warm or cold, as desired, with lemon wedges for squeezing over the top.

pasta salad with tuna, chilli & rocket

lime pickle & vegetable biryani

lime pickle & *vegetable* biryani

serves **4**

Q

V

Here is a speedy recipe in which vegetables are stir-fried with a spicy curry paste and cooked rice is then added. With the addition of a dollop of the lime pickle that is probably lurking at the back of your fridge, this is a stir-fry with a difference.

Put the pickle, onion, garlic and ginger in a food processor and process to make a paste. Heat the oil in a large saucepan. Add the paste and cook, stirring, for 2–3 minutes. Add the carrots and stir-fry for 2–3 minutes. Add the courgettes and stir-fry for 2 minutes, then turn off the heat.

Bring a large saucepan of water to the boil. Add the rice and cook for 8–10 minutes, until just tender. Add the rice vermicelli, if using, and cook for another 2–3 minutes, stirring well so that the vermicelli does not stick together and is soft and transparent. Drain well. Set the saucepan with the vegetables over high heat. Add the rice mixture and stir well until it takes on the golden colour of the curry paste. Stir in the mint and scatter with toasted cashews to serve.

2 tablespoon bottled lime pickle

1 onion, chopped

2 garlic cloves

2 teaspoons grated fresh ginger

2 tablespoons olive oil

2 carrots, cut into matchsticks

2 courgettes, cut into matchsticks

370 g basmati rice

50 g dried rice vermicelli, broken into shorter lengths (optional)

a large handful of fresh mint leaves

50 g toasted cashew nuts, chopped

pumpkin & *pea* risotto

125 g unsalted butter

3 tablespoons pumpkin seeds

¼–½ teaspoon ground chilli

about 1 litre hot Vegetable Stock (page 54)

1 large onion, finely chopped

500 g fresh butternut squash or pumpkin, peeled, deseeded and diced

300 g risotto rice

3 tablespoons freshly chopped mint

200 g fresh or frozen peas, cooked and drained

75 g Parmesan, grated

salt and black pepper

serves 6

V

A pretty orange colour speckled with sweet green peas, this risotto is a delight to eat – the peas pop in your mouth and the seeds give crunch. Take this opportunity to use some fresh peas from the garden, but if you're not lucky enough to have some (or they're not ready yet) frozen peas are heaven-sent.

Put half the butter in a saucepan, melt until foaming, then add the pumpkin seeds. Stir until the seeds begin to brown, then stir in the chilli, salt and pepper. Remove from the heat and keep them warm.

Put the stock in a saucepan and keep at a gentle simmer. Melt the remaining butter in a large, heavy saucepan and add the onion. Cook gently for 10 minutes until soft, golden and translucent but not browned. Add the squash or pumpkin, and cook, stirring constantly over the heat for 15 minutes until it begins to soften and disintegrate. Mash the pumpkin in the pan with a potato masher. Stir in the rice to coat with the butter and mashed pumpkin. Cook for a couple of minutes to toast the grains.

Begin adding the stock, a large ladle at a time, stirring gently until each ladle has almost been absorbed by the rice. The risotto should be kept at a bare simmer throughout cooking, so don't let the rice dry out – add more stock as necessary. Continue until the rice is tender and creamy, but the grains still firm. (This should take 15–20 minutes depending on the type of rice used – check the packet instructions.)

Taste and season well. Stir in the mint, peas and all the Parmesan. Cover and leave to rest for a couple of minutes so the risotto can relax, then serve immediately, sprinkled with the pumpkin seeds. You may like to add a little more hot stock to the risotto just before you serve to loosen it, but don't let it wait around too long or the rice will turn mushy.

green *herb* risotto
with *white wine & lemon*

You come home from work and you're craving something tasty but you haven't had time to get to the supermarket. The fridge is bare but for a splash of white wine, some spring onions and a medley of herbs leftover from last weekend's dinner. This is the recipe you need! A wonderfully light and fragrant risotto, made with the minimum of ingredients. If possible, try to use the more fragrant soft herbs – the more the merrier.

serves
4–6

V

Put the stock in a saucepan and keep at a gentle simmer. Melt half the butter in a large, heavy saucepan and add the spring onions. Cook gently for 3–5 minutes until soft. Pour in the wine, add half the lemon zest and boil hard until the wine has reduced and almost disappeared. This will remove the taste of raw alcohol. Add the rice and stir until well coated with butter and onions and heated through.

Begin to add the hot stock, a large ladle at a time, stirring until each ladle has been absorbed by the rice. Continue until the rice is tender and creamy, but the grains still firm. (This should take 15–20 minutes depending on the type of rice used – check the packet instructions.)

Taste and season well with salt and lots of black pepper. Stir in the remaining butter, the lemon zest, juice, herbs and Parmesan. Cover and leave to rest for a couple of minutes, then serve immediately.

about 1.5 litres hot Vegetable Stock (page 54)

125 g unsalted butter

8 spring onions, green and white parts, finely chopped

150 ml dry white wine

finely grated zest and juice of 1 large unwaxed lemon

500 g risotto rice

4 tablespoons freshly chopped herbs such as parsley, basil, marjoram and thyme

75 g Parmesan, grated

salt and black pepper

chicken liver risotto

175 g plump fresh chicken livers, trimmed and chopped

about 1.5 litres hot Chicken Stock (page 53) or Vegetable Stock (page 54)

125 g unsalted butter

2 shallots, finely chopped

1 celery stick, finely chopped

1 small carrot, finely chopped

3 tablespoons dry sherry

1 tablespoon sun-dried tomato paste or purée

400 g risotto rice

2 tablespoons salted capers, rinsed and chopped

3 tablespoons freshly chopped parsley

salt and black pepper

Cooking with chicken livers is often overlooked because they're considered old-fashioned or simply unpopular. But they are the ideal ingredient for a thrifty, meaty risotto and perfect married with a little of that dry sherry that's sitting undrunk at the back of the drinks cabinet.

Put the stock in a saucepan and keep at a gentle simmer. Melt half the butter in a large, heavy saucepan and add the shallots, celery and carrot. Cook gently for 6–8 minutes until soft, golden and translucent but not browned. Stir in the livers, then raise the heat until they are cooked and firm on the outside, soft and pink inside. Stir in the sherry and tomato paste and boil hard until the liquid has all but evaporated. Add the rice and stir until well coated with the butter and vegetables and heated through.

Begin adding the stock, a large ladle at a time, stirring gently so as not to break up the chicken livers too much, until each ladle has almost been absorbed by the rice. The risotto should be kept at a bare simmer throughout cooking, so don't let the rice dry out – add more stock as necessary. Continue until the rice is tender and creamy, but the grains still firm. (This should take 15–20 minutes depending on the type of rice used – check the packet instructions.)

Taste and season well. Beat in the remaining butter, the capers and parsley. Cover and leave to rest for a couple of minutes so the risotto can relax, then serve immediately. You may like to add a little more hot stock to the risotto just before you serve to loosen it, but don't let it wait around too long or the rice will turn mushy.

*baked courgette
& tomato risotto*

baked *courgette* & *tomato* risotto

This risotto is so simple, it cooks itself. Simple, fresh ingredients, a few quick stirs and dinner is ready to serve.

750 ml hot Vegetable Stock (page 54)

2 tablespoons olive oil

1 onion, chopped

1 garlic clove, chopped

330 g short-grain white rice

2 tablespoons fresh rosemary needles

2 courgettes, chopped

2 tomatoes, chopped

50 g unsalted butter

50 g Parmesan, finely grated

Preheat the oven to 200°C (400°C) Gas 6.

Put the stock in a large saucepan and set over low heat. Put the oil in an ovenproof, lidded casserole dish and set over low heat. Add the onion and garlic and fry gently for 2–3 minutes until the onion has softened. Add the rice and the rosemary and cook for a further minute before adding the courgettes. Stir for 1 minute, or until the rice becomes opaque, then add the tomatoes. Pour the hot stock into the casserole and stir well to remove any stuck-on bits and to combine all the ingredients. As soon as the liquid starts to simmer, cover with the lid and cook in the preheated oven for 30 minutes. Stir through the butter and half the Parmesan, then sprinkle the remaining Parmesan on top to serve.

smoked mussel & *leek* risotto

Though it tastes luxurious, the ingredients for this are store-cupboard staples. Tinned smoked mussels are a great standby.

about 1.5 litres hot Vegetable Stock (page 54)

125 g unsalted butter

1 large leek, finely sliced or chopped (all the white part and half of the green)

1 celery stick, finely chopped

400 g risotto rice

75 ml dry white vermouth

1 teaspoon freshly chopped tarragon

3 tins smoked mussels, 85 g each, drained

salt and black pepper

Put the stock in a saucepan and keep at a gentle simmer. Melt half the butter in a large, heavy saucepan and, when foaming, add the leek and celery and cook gently for 5 minutes until softened but not browned. Add the rice and stir until well coated with the butter and heated through. Pour in the vermouth and boil hard until it has reduced and almost disappeared. This will remove the taste of raw alcohol. Add the tarragon.

Begin adding the stock, a large ladle at a time, stirring gently until each ladle has almost been absorbed by the rice. The risotto should be kept at a bare simmer throughout cooking, so don't let the rice dry out – add more stock as necessary. Continue until the rice is tender and creamy, but the grains still firm. (This should take 15–20 minutes depending on the type of rice used – check the packet instructions.)

Taste and season well. Beat in the remaining butter and fold in the mussels. Cover and leave to rest for a couple of minutes so the risotto can relax and the seafood heat through, then serve immediately.

risotto primavera

1 litre hot Vegetable Stock
(page 54)

100 g unsalted butter

3 tablespoons olive oil

1 onion, diced

1 garlic clove, chopped

275 g risotto rice

625 g mixed green vegetables,
such as asparagus, broad
beans, dwarf beans, flat
beans, runner beans, green
cabbage, peas or spinach, all
chopped into even pieces

75 ml white wine

a handful of fresh flat leaf
parsley, chopped

125 g Parmesan, grated

salt and black pepper

serves 4

V

This is a very unfussy type of risotto. The trick is to use the freshest green spring vegetables you can lay your hands on.

Put the stock in a saucepan and keep at a gentle simmer. Heat the butter and olive oil in a large saucepan. Add the onion and garlic and cook over low heat for 5 minutes until softened and translucent. Add the rice, stirring with a wooden spoon to coat the grains thoroughly with butter and oil.

Add a ladle of stock to the rice, mix well and simmer. When the liquid has almost evaporated, add another ladle of stock to the saucepan and stir thoroughly until it bubbles away. Continue, stirring the risotto as often as possible and adding more stock as needed.

After the risotto has been cooking for 12 minutes, add all the vegetables and mix well. Add the remaining stock, white wine, salt and pepper. Cook, stirring, for a further 4–5 minutes, then mix in the parsley and Parmesan. Serve immediately.

mushroom risotto

1 litre hot Vegetable Stock
(page 54)

50 g dried mushrooms such as
chanterelles, morels,
shiitakes or porcini

25 g unsalted butter

1 tablespoon olive oil

1 garlic clove, crushed

1 onion, finely chopped

300 g risotto rice

75 ml dry white wine

75 g Parmesan, grated,
plus extra to serve

salt and black pepper

serves 4

V

Time to use up those dried wild mushrooms you've been storing (and failing to use) for all these months.

Put the stock and dried mushrooms in a saucepan and leave to soak for 10 minutes. Put the stock in a saucepan and keep at a gentle simmer. Strain the mushrooms and return the stock to the saucepan to keep hot.

Melt half the butter with the oil in a large saucepan. Add the garlic and onion and cook until softened and translucent. Add the rice and stir until all the grains are coated with butter and oil.

Add a ladle of hot stock to the rice and mix well. When the rice has absorbed the liquid, add another ladle of stock and stir well. Repeat with the remaining stock, cooking the risotto for 15–20 minutes until all the liquid has been absorbed. Meanwhile, chop the mushrooms if they are too big. Add the soaked mushrooms, white wine, the remaining butter and the Parmesan to the risotto. Season to taste and mix gently over the heat for 2 minutes. Serve with a separate dish of Parmesan to sprinkle over the top.

risotto primavera

orzo pilaf

orzo pilaf

This is a cross between a pilaf and a pasta bake, because the main ingredient is a little rice-shaped pasta called 'orzo'. Pop it all in the oven and let it do its thing. After 25 minutes, dinner will be ready.

Preheat the oven to 200°C (400°F) Gas 6.

Put the oil and onion in an ovenproof, lidded casserole dish over medium heat. Stir and cook until soft, 3–5 minutes. Add the garlic and orzo and stir until coated with the oil. Add the tomatoes, stock and parsley and stir well, breaking up the tomatoes with a wooden spoon.

Cover with the lid and bake in the preheated oven until the pasta is tender and most of the liquid has been absorbed, 20–25 minutes. Serve hot.

serves 4

M

2 tablespoons olive oil

1 onion, chopped

2 garlic cloves, crushed

250 g orzo pasta

400 g tinned chopped tomatoes

300 ml hot Chicken Stock (page 53)

a handful of fresh flat leaf parsley, chopped

salt and black pepper

chilli con carne

Simple dishes are often the best, and they don't come much simpler than this. You can add more or less cayenne pepper, depending on how hot you like your food.

Make the Bolognese as described on page 119, but also add the cayenne, paprika, wine and beans listed here before simmering for 1 hour.

Just before serving, stir in the coriander and serve with bread or boiled rice and a bowl of guacamole.

serves 4–6

M

1 quantity Bolognese (page 119, but see method here)

1 tablespoon cayenne pepper

1 tablespoon paprika

1 glass of red wine

800 g tinned red kidney beans, drained and rinsed

a handful of fresh coriander, chopped

bread or boiled rice, to serve

guacamole, to serve

lemony chicken with spring onions & pine nut couscous

60 g plain flour

1 chicken, about 1.6 kg, cut into 10 pieces

125 ml olive oil

12 spring onions

3 garlic cloves, chopped

1 unwaxed lemon, thickly sliced

125 ml white wine

125 ml lemon juice

125 ml hot Chicken Stock (page 53)

1 tablespoon light soy sauce

salt and black pepper

Pine nut couscous

2 tablespoons olive oil

25 g pine nuts

280 g couscous

375 ml hot Chicken Stock (page 53)

serves
4

M

With ingredients like lemon and soy sauce, you could be forgiven for thinking this is Chinese but the couscous brings it very much into the realms of North Africa. The technique of frying the couscous in a little oil with nuts is not entirely traditional but is foolproof. You could also use aromatic spices like paprika and cumin.

Season the flour with salt and pepper and put it in a clean plastic bag. Add half the chicken pieces and shake to coat them in the seasoned flour. Repeat with the remaining chicken pieces and set aside until needed.

Heat the olive oil in a large frying pan over medium/high heat. Add the spring onions and stir-fry for 4 minutes, until softened and silky. Remove the spring onions from the pan and set aside. Add half of the chicken to the pan and cook in batches for 4–5 minutes, turning each piece often, until golden brown all over. Transfer the browned chicken to a plate and repeat to cook the remaining chicken.

Pour off all but 1 tablespoon of oil from the pan, leaving any sediment in the pan. Add the garlic and lemon and cook for 1 minute, stirring well to combine with any of the cooked on bits on the bottom of the pan. Add the wine and leave to sizzle for 1 minute, then add the lemon juice, chicken stock and soy sauce and bring to the boil. Return the chicken to the pan and cook for 20 minutes. Turn each piece of chicken, then put the spring onions on top of the chicken. Cover the pan with cooking foil and cook for a further 20 minutes, until the chicken is cooked through. Stir to evenly combine the chicken and any of the cooking juices with the leeks. Cover the pan and set aside while cooking the couscous.

To make the pine nut couscous, put the olive oil and pine nuts in a saucepan and cook over high heat, stirring constantly, until the nuts begin to turn golden. Add the couscous and stir for 1 minute, then add the stock which will boil rapidly – quickly stir a couple of times. Turn the heat off, cover with a tight-fitting lid and leave to stand for 10 minutes. Fluff the couscous with a fork and cover again for 5 minutes. Fluff again to separate as many grains as possible and serve with the lemony chicken.

winter vegetable tagine

winter *vegetable* tagine

The rather heavy, pungent spices here go so well with the full-flavoured vegetables, which should be chopped into big chunks.

Heat the oil in a heavy-based saucepan and cook the onion and garlic over high heat for 2–3 minutes. Add all of the spices and cook for 2 minutes, until aromatic but not burning. Add 750 ml water and the tomatoes and season well. Bring to the boil, add the carrot and parsnip and cook for 30 minutes. Add the turnip, sweet potato and apple and cook for 20–30 minutes, until all the vegetables are soft, then stir in the mint.

Meanwhile, put the couscous in a large heatproof bowl with the butter. Pour over 375 ml boiling water, quickly stir once or twice, then cover with clingfilm and leave for 15 minutes. Stir the couscous again with a fork and cover for a further 5 minutes. Finally fluff the couscous with a fork to separate as many grains as possible. Serve with the tagine spooned over.

3 tablespoons olive oil

1 onion, chopped

2 garlic cloves, chopped

½ teaspoon turmeric

½ teaspoon paprika

1 teaspoon ground cumin

1 cinnamon stick

400 g tinned chopped tomatoes

1 large carrot, chopped

1 parsnip, chopped

1 turnip, chopped

125 g sweet potato, cubed

1 green apple, peeled, cored and cut into 8 wedges

a small handful of fresh mint, roughly chopped

280 g couscous

1 tablespoon unsalted butter

salt and black pepper

Moroccan-style roasted *vegetables*

This roasted vegetable couscous is spicy and satisfying.

Preheat the oven to 200°C (400°F) Gas 6.

Put the onion, potato, pepper, leek and garlic on a non-stick baking tray or in a small roasting tin. Pour the olive oil over the top, add the chilli flakes and use your hands to toss the vegetables until they are coated with the oil mixture. Place the tray or tin in the preheated oven and cook for about 20–25 minutes, or until golden and tender.

Meanwhile, put the couscous in a large bowl and pour over the hot vegetable stock or water. Cover and set aside until the couscous swells and absorbs all the liquid, about 10 minutes.

Use a fork to fluff up the couscous, then add the roasted vegetables and mint sprigs. Add a little lemon juice and season to taste. Serve immediately whilst still warm.

175 g red onion, cut into wedges

175 g sweet potato, cubed

175 g red pepper, deseeded and chopped

175 g leek, chopped

2 garlic cloves, halved

2 tablespoons olive oil

½ teaspoon dried chilli flakes

150 g couscous

300 ml hot Vegetable Stock (page 54) or water

a handful of fresh mint

lemon juice, to taste

salt and black pepper

chilli & garlic steamed mushrooms with polenta

serves
4

V

12 field mushrooms

65 ml dry white wine

65 ml olive oil

2 large red chillies, deseeded and chopped

2 garlic cloves, chopped

3 tablespoons freshly chopped flat leaf parsley

Crisp polenta

500 ml milk

150 g instant polenta

1 teaspoon salt

75 g unsalted butter

50 g Parmesan, finely grated

250 ml olive oil

a vegetable steamer, ideally bamboo

The flavours here are very Italian, but you could easily swap the parsley for coriander, add a splash of light soy sauce and suddenly find yourself in Asia. Almost any cultivated mushroom works here, but do try the recipe with fresh shiitake mushrooms if you decide to go the Asian route.

Cut any large stalks off the mushrooms and discard. Put the mushroom caps in a non-metallic, flat dish with the wine, oil, chillies and garlic and use your hands to toss the mushrooms around until coated with the marinade. Cover and marinate for 1 hour.

Sit the dish of mushrooms inside a large steamer – a large Asian bamboo steamer is ideal. Set the steamer over a large saucepan of boiling water, cover and steam for 20 minutes until tender.

Lightly oil a baking tray. Put the milk in a saucepan with 500 ml water and set over medium heat. Bring just to the boil, then pour the polenta into the saucepan in a steady stream, whisking constantly to avoid any lumps. Add the salt and stir for 5 minutes until the polenta is soft. Remove from the heat, add the butter and Parmesan and beat until the mixture is smooth. Spread the polenta out on the oiled baking tray and put in the refrigerator to chill.

When completely cold, cut the polenta into 12 squares. Put the oil in a frying pan set over high heat, add the polenta slices and fry for 4–5 minutes on each side until golden and crisp. Remove them from the pan and drain any excess oil on kitchen paper. Put 3 slices of polenta onto each of 4 serving plates, spoon the mushrooms and juices over the top and sprinkle with the parsley to serve.

gnocchi with *herbs* & *semolina*

Soft and golden, these gnocchi are good with roasts. Consider keeping a stash of semolina – it's a good storecupboard standby.

serves
4–6

V

Pour the milk into a saucepan and whisk in the semolina. Bring slowly to the boil, stirring, until it really thickens – about 10 minutes (it should be quite thick). Beat in half the Parmesan, half the butter, the egg yolks, mustard, sage and parsley. Season to taste. Line a baking tray with clingfilm, then spread the mixture onto it to a depth of 1.25 cm. Leave to set, about 2 hours.

Preheat the oven to 200°C (400°F) Gas 6.

Cut the set mixture into rounds with the biscuit cutter. Spread the chopped trimmings in the bottom of the ovenproof dish. Dot with some of the remaining butter and sprinkle with a little Parmesan. Arrange the gnocchi shapes in a single layer over the trimmings. Dot with the remaining butter and Parmesan. Bake in the preheated oven for 20–25 minutes until golden and crusty. Leave to stand for 5 minutes before serving.

1 litre milk

250 g semolina

175 g Parmesan, grated

125 g unsalted butter

2 egg yolks

1 tablespoon Dijon mustard

2 tablespoons freshly chopped sage

3 tablespoons freshly chopped flat leaf parsley

salt and black pepper

a 4.5-cm round biscuit cutter

an ovenproof dish, 20 x 25 cm, well greased

oven bakes, pies & roasts

*baked ham with
layered potatoes*

baked *ham* with layered *potatoes*

Family meals don't come much simpler than this. For easier carving, ask your butcher to bone the ham joint for you.

Preheat the oven to 200°C (400°F) Gas 6.

If the ham joint is salty, cover it in cold water and leave to soak for 1 hour. Drain and pat dry with kitchen paper. Wrap the ham loosely in foil and put in a roasting tin. Bake for 1 hour 20 minutes (or 40 minutes per 500 g).

Meanwhile, put a layer of potatoes (overlapping slightly) in the prepared dish, top with a layer of onions and season. Continue making layers, finishing with a layer of the potatoes. Push the layers down firmly with the palms of your hands. Pour the hot stock into the dish, brush the top with melted butter and cover with foil.

Bake the potatoes at the top of the preheated oven with the ham for 50 minutes, then remove the foil and cook for a further 30 minutes. The top will be golden and crunchy and the potatoes soft when a knife is inserted.

serves
6

M

1-kg ham joint, boned

900 g potatoes, thinly sliced

1–2 onions, thinly sliced

250 ml hot Chicken Stock (page 53)

25 g unsalted butter, melted

salt and black pepper

a shallow baking dish, 20 cm in diameter, greased

pizza with *potatoes*

Of course, you can put any topping you like on a shop-bought pizza base, but this is fuss-free and needs so few ingredients to make it delicious.

Preheat the oven to 220°C (425°F) Gas 7 and put 2 baking trays in to heat up.

Put the potato slices, olive oil, garlic, rosemary needles and salt into a large bowl and toss together to coat.

Spread the potato mixture evenly over both pizzas. Remove the trays from the oven and slide 1 pizza onto each one. Sprinkle with more olive oil and salt if required and bake for 15–20 minutes, or until the potatoes are tender and the pizzas lightly golden and crisp.

makes
2

2 x 23–25-cm ready-made pizza bases

500 g waxy potatoes, very thinly sliced

2 tablespoons olive oil

4 garlic cloves, crushed

2 sprigs of fresh rosemary, needles pulled off

1 teaspoon salt

mushroom, spinach & potato bake

1 kg floury potatoes, chopped

125 ml whole milk

a pinch of grated nutmeg

125 g unsalted butter, cubed

500 g small chestnut mushrooms, left whole and stalks removed

4 garlic cloves, chopped

4 spring onions, cut into 2-cm lengths

1 kg spinach, chopped

200 g fontina, Gruyère or Cheddar, cubed

salt and black pepper

serves 4–6

V

This is by no means a token vegetarian option – it is hearty, comforting and tasty, and will satisfy the hungriest of guests.

Put the potatoes in a large saucepan of lightly salted boiling water and boil for about 12–15 minutes, until tender but not falling apart. Drain well, return to the warm pan and roughly mash. Add the milk and nutmeg and season to taste. Beat until smooth. Stir through half the butter. Spoon about one-third of the mixture into a baking dish.

Preheat the oven to 180°C (350°F) Gas 4.

Heat half the remaining butter in a large frying pan. Add the mushrooms, garlic and spring onions and gently fry for about 10 minutes, until golden. Spoon over the potato mixture in the baking dish. Heat the remaining butter in the frying pan and cook the spinach for 5 minutes, stirring often, until just wilted. Season to taste and spoon over the mushrooms in the baking dish. Spoon the remaining mashed potatoes on top and scatter over the cheese. Bake in the preheated oven for 30 minutes, or until the cheese is golden.

Lancashire hotpot

2 tablespoons olive oil

800 g lamb neck fillet, cut into 5-cm pieces

1 onion, diced

2 carrots, diced

4 celery sticks, diced

2 leeks, thinly sliced

2 tablespoons plain flour

1 tablespoon Worcestershire sauce

800 g potatoes (unpeeled), very thinly sliced

salt and black pepper

serves 4–6

M

Inspired by thrift, this dish has transcended its humble origins and become a firm favourite around the world.

Heat the olive oil in a large, ovenproof casserole dish, add the lamb and brown all over. Transfer to a plate. Reduce the heat under the casserole, add all the vegetables then sauté for 10 minutes, stirring frequently. Remove the casserole from the heat, add the meat, then sprinkle in the flour and mix well. Pour in just enough hot water to cover the meat and vegetables, stir well and return to the heat.

Preheat the oven to 180°C (350°F) Gas 4.

Bring the casserole to the boil, stirring frequently as the gravy thickens. Season and add the Worcestershire sauce. Remove from the heat. Layer the potatoes carefully over the meat and vegetables, covering them completely. Place in the oven and cook for 2 hours.

mushroom, spinach
& potato bake

winter *vegetable* gratin

This is a great way to use up any combination of cold-weather root vegetables, such as swede, which is often overlooked.

serves
6

V

Preheat the oven to 180°C (350°F) Gas 4 and lightly grease a baking dish.

Bring a large saucepan of lightly salted water to the boil and add the celeriac, carrot, parsnip, swede and potatoes. Cook for 10 minutes, drain well and transfer the vegetables to a large bowl.

Put the cream, garlic and mustard powder in a small saucepan. Cook, stirring constantly, for about 10 minutes until the mixture is thick and coats the back of a spoon. Season to taste and pour over the vegetables. Toss to combine and spoon the mixture into the baking dish.

Put the breadcrumbs, Parmesan and marjoram in a bowl and mix together. Sprinkle the breadcrumbs over the vegetables and drizzle the melted butter over the top. Cook in the preheated oven for 40 minutes, until golden and the mixture around the edge of the baking dish has formed a golden crust.

200 g celeriac, cut into 3-cm pieces

1 carrot, sliced

1 parsnip, sliced

1 small swede, cut into chunks

2 potatoes, cut into 3–cm pieces

250 ml single cream

1 garlic clove, crushed

1 teaspoon mustard powder

50 g breadcrumbs

2 tablespoons grated Parmesan

1 teaspoon dried marjoram

25 g unsalted butter, melted

salt and black pepper

pumpkin & *rice* gratin

This gratin contains rice, which makes it substantial enough to be a meal on its own, served with a green salad.

serves
6–8

V

Put the pumpkin in a large saucepan with 2 tablespoons of the olive oil, a pinch of salt and 250 ml water. Cook over low heat, stirring often and adding more water as necessary, until soft, about 20–30 minutes.

Preheat the oven to 200°C (400°F) Gas 6 and grease a baking dish.

Put the rice and the remaining oil in another saucepan and cook, stirring to coat the grains. Add 250 ml water, a pinch of salt and the thyme and bring to the boil. Cover and simmer until almost tender, about 10 minutes, then drain and discard the thyme.

Mix the breadcrumbs with the parsley and a pinch of salt. Squash the cooked pumpkin into a coarse purée with a spoon and stir in the rice and crème fraîche. Spoon the pumpkin mixture into the baking dish, spreading evenly. Sprinkle the cheese over the top, then follow with a layer of the breadcrumbs. Bake in the preheated oven until browned, 20–30 minutes.

1.5 kg pumpkin, peeled, deseeded and cubed

3 tablespoons olive oil

100 g long-grain white rice

a sprig of fresh thyme

3 tablespoons breadcrumbs

a small handful of fresh flat leaf parsley, finely chopped

3 tablespoons crème fraîche

75 g Gruyère or Cheddar cheese, grated

salt and black pepper

stuffed *tomatoes*

2 tablespoons olive oil

4 shallots, finely chopped

3 large garlic cloves, crushed

100 g bacon, finely chopped

3 tablespoons dry white wine

12 large tomatoes

375 g minced beef

1 egg

4 tablespoons breadcrumbs

½ teaspoon herbes de provence

a handful of fresh flat leaf parsley, finely chopped

salt and black pepper

serves
4–6

M

This recipe calls for leftover beef from a stew – home economy at its best. It's also nice if you mix leftovers, like lamb and pork, with the beef.

Preheat the oven to 200°C (400°F) Gas 6 and grease a baking dish.

Heat the olive oil in a frying pan. Add the shallots and garlic and cook until softened but not browned, 3–5 minutes. Add the bacon and fry until just beginning to brown, 3–5 minutes. Stir in the wine and cook until evaporated. Transfer to a bowl and leave to cool.

Slice off the tops of the tomatoes and set the tops aside. Carefully deseed with a spoon. Pat the insides dry with kitchen paper and season. Set aside.

Add the beef to the shallot mixture, then stir in the egg, breadcrumbs, herbs, parsley and 1 teaspoon salt. Cook a small piece of the stuffing mixture in a frying pan and taste for seasoning, adding more salt if needed.

Fill the tomato shells with the beef mixture, mounding it at the top. Replace the tomato tops and arrange apart in the baking dish. Cook in the preheated oven until cooked through and browned, about 30 minutes.

stuffed *peppers*

4 long peppers, halved lengthways and deseeded

200 g mushrooms, chopped

150 g mozzarella cheese, drained and cubed

2 garlic cloves, crushed

3 tablespoons olive oil

75 g olives stuffed with anchovies, chopped

½ tablespoon paprika

salt and black pepper

serves
4

F

Long, thin, sweet Romano peppers are best for this easy dish. However, if they aren't in season, ordinary peppers can be used although a little extra filling may be needed, as they tend to be larger.

Preheat the oven to 180°C (350°F) Gas 4 and grease a baking tray.

Put the pepper halves skin side down onto the baking tray.

Put the mushrooms, mozzarella, garlic, oil, olives and paprika into a bowl. Season to taste and mix well. Spoon the mixture into the peppers. Cook near the top of the preheated oven for 30 minutes. Serve hot or warm.

stuffed tomatoes

honeyed chicken wings

honeyed *chicken* wings

Here is a fantastic recipe for sweet, sticky, finger-licking chicken wings, served warm – they are so effortless and yet everyone will be asking for more!

Preheat the oven to 200°C (400°F) Gas 6 and grease a roasting tin.

Put the chicken wings into the roasting tin and cook in the preheated oven for 40 minutes, turning them after 20 minutes so they brown evenly all over.

Meanwhile, put the honey and sweet chilli sauce into a small saucepan. Season to taste and bring to the boil. Pour the sauce over the chicken, mix well and leave to cool. Serve with radishes, if using.

serves
8

Q

M

16 chicken wings

200 ml clear honey

100 ml sweet chilli sauce

salt and black pepper

a bunch of radishes, trimmed, to serve (optional)

lemon-spiced chicken

lemon-spiced *chicken*

Thighs are the best choice for this lemony, spicy marinade, because they stay tender and moist, though there's nothing to stop you from using a whole chicken cut into pieces. It's good to serve this with something to soak up the juices, such as rice.

Preheat the oven to 200°C (400°F) Gas 6.

Trim any excess fat from the chicken pieces. Put the chicken in a baking dish large enough to hold them comfortably (or divide between 2 dishes). Put the oil, lemon juice, cumin, paprika, chilli flakes, oregano, thyme, salt and pepper in a bowl and mix well. Pour over the chicken and turn to coat well. Cover and set aside for at least 30 minutes, or refrigerate for 6–8 hours.

Make sure all the chicken pieces are skin side up in the dish and roast in the preheated oven until browned and cooked through, 50–60 minutes. Serve immediately with the pan juices.

serves
4

M

12–16 chicken pieces, preferably thighs (allow 3–4 per person)

5 tablespoons olive oil

juice of 2 lemons

1 tablespoon ground cumin

1 teaspoon Spanish smoked paprika

½ teaspoon chilli flakes

1 teaspoon dried oregano

a small bunch of thyme sprigs, fresh or dried

2 teaspoons salt

1 teaspoon black pepper

chicken & *sweet potatoes*

Fusing ingredients from different culinary regions doesn't always work, but here it's perfect – Western olives, pimento and basil mixed with Eastern soy sauce, lemon and honey. The sweet potato base mops up all the cooking juices from the chicken.

Preheat the oven to 200°C (400°F) Gas 6.

Heat 4 tablespoons of the oil in a large frying pan, add the sweet potatoes and sauté until lightly browned. Transfer to an ovenproof casserole dish.

Add the remaining oil to the frying pan, add the chicken legs and sauté until browned all over. Put them on top of the sweet potatoes in the dish.

Put the olives, wine, honey, basil, garlic, soy sauce, lemon zest and juice into a food processor or blender and purée until smooth. Pour the mixture over the chicken.

Transfer to the preheated oven and cook for about 30 minutes, or until the casserole comes to the boil, then reduce the heat to 150°C (300°F) Gas 2 and simmer for 30 minutes, or until the chicken is tender.

serves
4

M

6 tablespoons olive oil

2 sweet potatoes, about 1 kg, cut into 1-cm rounds

4 chicken legs (thighs and drumsticks)

150 g pimento-stuffed green olives

125 ml dry white wine

4 tablespoons honey

a handful of fresh basil

4 garlic cloves, crushed

4 tablespoons soy sauce

finely grated zest and juice of 2 unwaxed lemons

cider pork with potatoes & apples

90 g unsalted butter

2 onions, sliced

1 tablespoon sunflower oil

1 pork middle leg roast, about 1.75 kg

1.5 litres dry cider

2 sprigs of fresh thyme

800 g new potatoes, halved lengthways

5 tart apples, such as Braeburn or Cox's, peeled, cored and sliced

125 ml double cream

salt and black pepper

serves
4

M

A good dish for all the family, as children often enjoy sweet things to accompany their meat.

Preheat the oven to 150°C (300°F) Gas 2.

Melt one-third of the butter in a large ovenproof casserole dish. Add the onions and cook gently until softened but not browned, about 5 minutes. Remove the onions. Add the oil, raise the heat, add the pork and cook until browned all over. Remove and season well. Add some of the cider, heat and scrape the bottom of the pan. Return the meat, onions, remaining cider and thyme. Season lightly and bring to the boil. Boil for 1 minute, skim off any foam that rises to the surface, then lower the heat, cover and cook in the preheated oven for 4 hours. Turn the pork regularly, and taste and adjust the seasoning halfway through cooking.

One hour before the end of the cooking time, add the potatoes and continue cooking. Remove from the oven, transfer the pork and potatoes to a plate and cover with foil. Cook the sauce over high heat to reduce slightly, about 10–15 minutes. Melt the remaining butter in a frying pan, add the apples and cook over high heat until browned and tender, 5–10 minutes. Stir the cream into the sauce before spooning over the apples, pork and potatoes.

red-cooked pork

1 kg pork spareribs, loin or shoulder, in the piece

Red stock

500 ml Chinese rice wine

750 ml Chicken Stock (page 53)

500 ml dark soy sauce

2 tablespoons rice vinegar

2 cinnamon sticks

3 cm fresh ginger, sliced

zest of 1 tangerine or orange

2 whole star anise

6 spring onions

serves
6–8

M

'Red-cooking' is a braising method used for duck, chicken or large pieces of pork. This dish uses a great deal of soy, but the stock can be used again and again (freeze between uses).

Preheat the oven to 180°C (350°F) Gas 4.

Put all the stock ingredients into a large ovenproof casserole dish and bring to the boil. Add the pork, return to the boil, then simmer on top of the stove or in the preheated oven for 45 minutes if using pork loin, or 1½ hours if using pork shoulder or spareribs. When the meat is very tender, carefully lift it out onto on a wooden board and, using a Chinese cleaver, cut it into thick slices or bite-sized chunks. Serve with other Chinese dishes such as noodles, stir-fried vegetables or steamed rice.

cider pork with
potatoes & apples

Tuscan *pork* & *bean* casserole

A 'hand' of pork is part of the shoulder of the animal. It is much the best part for roasting or braising, as it has just the right amount of fat, whereas the leg is so lean as to make it difficult to keep moist. Anyway, a certain amount of fat is needed in this dish to moisten the beans – or perhaps it's the other way round and the beans are needed to mop up the juices. Either way, it makes for a scrumptious dinner but remember that you will need to soak the beans overnight before you start.

Put the dried beans in a bowl, cover with water and leave to soak overnight.

The next day, preheat the oven to 170°C (325°F) Gas 3.

Drain the beans, transfer to a saucepan, cover with water again and bring to the boil. Drain and discard this water then reserve the beans.

Heat the oil in a large, lidded ovenproof casserole dish, then stir in the carrots, onions, turnips, thyme, bay leaf, peppercorns and garlic. Sauté gently until softened but not browned.

Meanwhile, cut the rind off the pork and reserve it. Add the pork, its rind, the bacon chunks and the drained beans to the casserole. Cover with water, season and bring to the boil on top of the stove. Transfer to the preheated oven and simmer for 1½ hours, or until the beans are tender.

After 1 hour, taste and adjust the seasoning, then add the potatoes for the last 30 minutes and the green beans for the last 5 minutes.

To serve, remove and discard the pork rind, lift the meat onto a dish and carve into thick slices. Add the vegetables and beans to the dish and serve with a separate small jug of the cooking juices.

serves
4

M

250 g dried cannellini beans

4 tablespoons olive oil

350 g carrots, cut into 3-cm pieces

4 onions (peeled)

4 small turnips

a sprig of fresh thyme

1 dried bay leaf

6 peppercorns

6 garlic cloves, or to taste

2 kg hand of pork

250 g rindless smoked streaky bacon in the piece, cut into chunks

750 g small potatoes (peeled)

250 g green beans

salt and black pepper

choucroute *garnie*

1 kg bottled sauerkraut,
1 litre by volume

5 tablespoons unsalted butter

250 g streaky bacon, chopped

1 carrot, sliced

1 onion, sliced

1 dried bay leaf

2 sprigs of fresh thyme

6 black peppercorns

125 ml white wine

500 ml hot Chicken Stock
(page 53)

4 pork neck cutlets

8 frankfurters, roughly
chopped

salt and black pepper

serves
4

M

Try a choucroute at least once in your life and you'll be hooked. It reheats very well and doesn't mind waiting, so cook more than you need and have it twice. Jazz it up with duck confit or roast goose for an extra-special treat (home-cooked or from a French deli). Make sure you use butter, not olive oil for frying because olive oil provides completely the wrong flavour. And finally, choucroute is traditionally served on a large platter in the middle of the table. Since Alsace is its original home, a cold beer would be a fantastic accompaniment.

Preheat the oven to 170°C (325°F) Gas 3.

Drain the sauerkraut, empty it into a large saucepan and cover with water. Stir well, empty into a colander, then drain.

Heat 3 tablespoons of the butter in a large, lidded ovenproof casserole dish, add the bacon, carrot, onion, herbs and peppercorns and cook gently for 5 minutes. Add the wine, bring to the boil and reduce by half.

Add the stock and stir in the drained sauerkraut. Cover with a lid, bring to the boil and cook in the preheated oven for 2 hours.

Meanwhile, heat the butter in a frying pan, add the pork cutlets, season and sauté until browned. Tuck the pork cutlets into the sauerkraut for the last hour. Add the frankfurters for the final 5 minutes.

braised beef brisket
with carrots

braised *beef* brisket with *carrots*

This humble French culinary masterpiece rates high on the scale of life's little pleasures.

Preheat the oven to 150°C (300°F) Gas 2.

Heat 1 tablespoon of the oil in a large, lidded ovenproof casserole dish. Add the brisket and cook until browned on all sides. Transfer to a plate and sprinkle generously with salt. Heat the remaining oil in the casserole, add the carrots and 1 teaspoon salt and cook, stirring occasionally until brown, 3–5 minutes. Remove and set aside.

Put the lardons and onion in the casserole and cook over high heat until browned, 3–5 minutes. Add the garlic, bay leaf, thyme, celery, beef and carrots. Pour in the wine and add water almost to cover. Bring to the boil, skim, then cover with a lid and cook in the preheated oven for 3 hours. Turn the meat over at least once during cooking. Sprinkle with pepper and serve.

2 tablespoons olive oil

1.5 kg rolled brisket

1.5 kg carrots, scrubbed and left whole

150 g bacon lardons

1 onion, halved and sliced

2 garlic cloves, crushed

1 fresh bay leaf

a sprig of fresh thyme

1 small leafy celery stick

500 ml dry white wine

salt and black pepper

braised *lamb* shanks with *orange*

Restaurants often serve up divinely cooked lamb shanks, which makes you believe that they must be difficult to cook, or expensive. Amazingly, they are neither, and just need time in the oven to become meltingly tender.

Preheat the grill until very hot. Brush the shanks with most of the olive oil and season well, then grill, turning as necessary until well browned.

Preheat the oven to 180°C (350°F) Gas 4.

Heat the remaining oil in a lidded, ovenproof casserole dish, add the garlic and brown gently without burning. Add the shanks, orange juice, wine and lemon zest. Bring to the boil on the stove, cover with a lid, then transfer to the preheated oven and cook for 1 hour, or until the meat pulls away from the bones. Transfer the shanks to a plate and cover with foil. Transfer the casserole to the stove. Add the marmalade to the casserole, stir until well blended, bring to the boil and simmer until reduced to a glaze. Return the shanks to the casserole and turn in the glaze until well coated. Transfer the shanks to plates. Add the stock to the casserole, stir to scrape up the flavoured bits left in the pan, then spoon over the shanks and serve.

4 lamb shanks

4 tablespoons olive oil

3 garlic cloves, sliced

about 250 ml orange juice

125 ml dry white wine

zest of 1 unwaxed lemon, removed with a zester or potato peeler

3 tablespoons bitter orange marmalade

125 ml hot Chicken Stock (page 53) or water

salt and black pepper

Irish carbonnade

2 tablespoons peanut or sunflower oil

750 g skirt steak or casserole beef, cut into 3-cm pieces

3 tablespoons sugar

1 onion, chopped

2 tablespoons plain flour

12 shallots

500 ml hot Beef Stock (page 53)

375 ml stout, such as Guinness

2 tablespoons red wine vinegar

3 cloves

2 dried bay leaves

salt and black pepper

serves
4

M

Carbonnades are native to Belgium and northern France, where they are always flavoured with beer. A good Irish stout works even better. A carbonnade uses caramelized sugar to sweeten the gravy. In this version, stout gives an extra touch of bitterness and this must be corrected to be pleasing. Lots of sweet shallots or pickling onions will also add to the sweetness. Serve with piles of creamy mashed potatoes and sautéed mushrooms, if you like.

Preheat the oven to 170°C (325°F) Gas 3.

Heat the oil in a large frying pan. Season the meat, add to the pan and sauté until browned on all sides. Transfer to a large, lidded ovenproof casserole dish.

Add the sugar to the frying pan and cook until it becomes a good chestnut colour. Add the onion, flour and shallots and mix well for about 30 seconds. Stir in the stock and stout. Bring to the boil and cook for 1 minute. Add the vinegar, cloves, bay leaves and a little more seasoning, then pour it all over the meat in the casserole. Mix well.

Cover the casserole and simmer very gently in the preheated oven for 1½–2 hours. Remove from the oven and pour off the liquid into a separate saucepan or frying pan. Bring to the boil and simmer to reduce the liquid to a coating consistency. Return it to the casserole and serve with creamy mashed potatoes and sautéed mushrooms, or any other accompaniments of your choice.

shepherd's pie

Old-school, traditional fare like shepherd's pie never goes out of style. Everyone loves it! If you want to make this a little smarter, say for a thrifty dinner party, bake it in individual ovenproof dishes. Next time you make this, you could use beef or pork mince as an alternative to the lamb. Try adding some thinly sliced leeks or finely chopped fennel bulbs when you are cooking the onions.

serves
6

M

2 tablespoons olive oil

125 g unsalted butter

2 large onions, chopped

2 carrots, grated

2 celery sticks, chopped

750 g minced lamb

1 litre hot Beef Stock (page 53)

2½ tablespoons cornflour

a large handful of fresh flat leaf parsley, finely chopped

1 kg floury potatoes, quartered or halved, depending on size

85 ml milk

salt and black pepper

Heat the olive oil and 1 tablespoon of the butter in large, heavy-based frying pan set over high heat. When the butter has melted and is sizzling, add the onions and cook for 5 minutes, until golden. Add the carrots and celery and cook for a further 5 minutes. Add the lamb and cook for 10 minutes, until it has browned, stirring often to break up any large clumps.

Put the cornflour in a small bowl and stir in 65 ml of the stock. Add the remaining stock to the pan with the lamb and cook for 10 minutes, letting the stock boil and reduce a little. Add the cornflour mixture to the pan and cook, stirring constantly, until the liquid thickens to a gravy. Stir in the parsley, season well and set aside.

Preheat the oven to 180°C (350°F) Gas 4.

Put the potatoes in a large saucepan of lightly salted boiling water. Cook for 10 minutes, until they are just starting to break up and the water is cloudy. Drain well and return to the warm pan. Add the remaining butter and the milk and season to taste. Roughly mash so that you leave the potatoes with a chunky texture.

Spoon the lamb into a baking dish and spread the mashed potatoes over the top. Cook in the preheated oven for about 40–45 minutes, until the potato is crisp and golden brown.

oxtail in *red wine*

7 tablespoons olive oil

3 tablespoons plain flour

2 large onions, sliced

2 oxtails, about 2 kg, jointed cleanly into sections, trimmed of fat (ask your butcher to do this for you)

2 carrots, cut into large pieces

4 tomatoes, chopped

2–3 sprigs of fresh thyme

1 celery stick, sliced

3 dried bay leaves

10 black peppercorns

150 ml brandy

1 bottle red wine, 750 ml

1.75 litres hot Beef Stock (page 53)

salt and black pepper

freshly cooked vegetables, such as baby carrots, turnips and parsnips and green vegetables, such as broccoli, to serve

Oxtail is much under-used in cooking – it tends to be regarded with suspicion – but makes a rich stew and its natural gelatin gives the dish a delicious, sticky, glutinous texture. However, it also has an excessive amount of fat on the biggest sections, most of which must be cut away before cooking and lifted off when the cooking is complete. You can also chill the casserole overnight and remove the fat when cold.

Preheat the oven to 150°C (300°F) Gas 2.

To make a roux, put 3 tablespoons of the olive oil in a small frying pan, add the flour and cook gently, stirring, until it becomes a nutty brown colour.

Heat another 3 tablespoons of the oil in a large ovenproof casserole dish, add the onion and sauté until golden. Add the smaller pieces of oxtail, carrots, tomatoes, thyme, celery, bay leaves and peppercorns. Fry until browned. Transfer to a bowl and keep everything warm.

Rinse the casserole, return to the heat and add the remaining oil. Add the larger pieces of oxtail and fry until browned on all sides. Pour off the fat.

Warm the brandy in a small saucepan, light with a match and pour over the meat. Shake the casserole gently, keeping the flame alight as long as possible to burn off all the alcohol.

Transfer the meat to the bowl of vegetables and add the wine to the casserole. Bring to the boil and cook until it becomes syrupy and almost disappears. Stir in the roux, then the stock. Bring to the boil, stirring all the time to make a sauce. Season, then gently mix in all the meat and vegetables. Transfer to the preheated oven and cook for at least 3 hours, or until the meat is falling off the bone.

Remove from the oven and set aside for about 10 minutes to let the fat rise to the surface. Spoon off as much fat as you can. Alternatively, leave to cool, then chill overnight.

About 1 hour before serving, remove any fat from the surface and reheat the stew, adding a little boiling water if the sauce has become too dry. Taste and adjust the seasoning. Transfer the large pieces of meat to a bowl and strain the gravy over. Discard the vegetables and any small bones. Gently return the stew to the casserole and top with your freshly cooked vegetables.

beef pie

Who doesn't love pie – hearty, warming and comforting on a horrible winter's night. What's more, this one is made with ready-made shortcrust pastry so all the hard work is done for you. All you need with it is mash and peas.

serves
4

M

500 g chuck steak, cut into bite-sized pieces

3 tablespoons plain flour

50 g unsalted butter

2 onions, chopped

2 tablespoons olive oil

250 ml beer

500 ml hot Beef Stock (page 53)

2 tablespoons Worcestershire sauce

1 tablespoon light soy sauce

350 g ready-made shortcrust pastry, defrosted if frozen

1 egg yolk, beaten with 1 tablespoon water

a ceramic pie dish

Put the beef in a colander. Sprinkle with the flour and use your hands to toss the pieces until they are coated in flour.

Heat the butter in a large, heavy-based saucepan set over medium/high heat. Add the onions and cook for 5 minutes, until golden. Remove from the pan and set aside. Add 1 tablespoon of the oil to the pan. Add half the beef and cook for 4–5 minutes, until browned all over. Remove from the pan and set aside. Add the remaining oil to the pan and repeat with all the remaining beef.

Add the beer, stock and sauces to the pan and bring to the boil. Return the beef to the pan, cook briefly, then reduce the heat to low. Cover and cook for 1 hour, stirring occasionally. Add the onions and increase the heat to high. Boil for about 15–20 minutes, until the gravy is thick and dark. Leave to cool completely before continuing with the rest of the recipe.

Preheat the oven to 200°C (400°F) Gas 6 and put a baking tray on the middle shelf of the oven to heat up.

Lightly flour a work surface. Roll the pastry out to a thickness of about 5 mm. Use a sharp knife to cut a circle slightly larger than the top of the pie dish. Re-roll the remaining pastry and use a knife to cut long strips about 1.5 cm wide. Brush some of the egg wash around the rim of the pie dish and press the pastry strips around the edge. Brush the pastry with egg wash and put the pastry lid on top. Use a fork to press down around the edge to seal and brush all over the remaining egg wash. Bake in the preheated oven for about 45–50 minutes, until the pastry is golden and crisp.

egg, bacon & spinach pie

500 g spinach

1 tablespoon unsalted butter

3 rashers of rindless, streaky bacon, cut into thin strips

1 onion, finely chopped

6 eggs, lightly beaten

50 g Parmesan, finely grated

1 egg, lightly beaten with 1 tablespoon cold water

Shortcrust pastry

250 g plain flour

150 g unsalted butter, cubed

1 egg yolk

a loose-based tart tin, 20 cm in diameter, lightly greased

Pies are as good outdoors as they are indoors. They transport well for picnics and leftovers will sit happily in the fridge for a couple of days so you can enjoy them as a snack or late supper. Unlike the pie on the previous page, this one requires home-made pastry but if you have a rainy weekend afternoon to kill, there's nothing homelier than making your own pastry.

Put the flour and butter into the bowl of a food processor and put the bowl into the freezer for 15 minutes. Lightly beat the egg yolk with 2 tablespoons water and refrigerate for 15 minutes. Process the butter and flour until the mixture looks like ground almonds, then add the egg yolk mixture and process for just a few seconds to combine. Tip the mixture into a bowl and use your hands to bring the dough together to form one large ball. It should be a bit crumbly. Wrap in clingfilm and refrigerate for 30 minutes.

Preheat the oven to 180°C (350°F) Gas 4. Wash the spinach and, leaving some of the water on the leaves, cook it in a large non-stick frying pan over high heat for 2 minutes, until wilted and emerald green in colour. You may need to cook it in batches. Transfer it to a colander and drain well. When cool enough to handle, use your hands to squeeze out as much moisture as possible from the spinach and place it in a large bowl.

Heat the butter in the frying pan over high heat and, when sizzling, add the bacon and onion. Cook for 5 minutes until golden. Spoon the mixture into the bowl with the spinach. Add the eggs and Parmesan and season well. Stir to combine.

Put the greased tart tin on a baking tray. Cut about two-thirds from the ball of dough and roll it out between two layers of greaseproof paper. Line the bottom of the tart tin with the pastry. Spoon the spinach mixture on top of the pastry base. Roll the remaining pastry into a circle slightly larger than the tart tin and place this on top of the pie, allowing any excess pastry to hang over the edge. Gently press down around the edges to seal. Brush the egg and water mixture over the pie and cook in the preheated oven for 1 hour until golden brown.

Leave the pie to cool for 10–15 minutes before serving.

traditional Greek *cheese* pie

The effort it takes to make these fantastic pies is offset by the size of the ingredients list – the chances are that all you will need to buy is the feta. The recipe makes 2 generous pies, which will feed 8–12 people so it's great for taking on a picnic or for casual entertaining. It is sensational eaten straight out of the frying pan.

250 g plain flour

a pinch of salt

olive oil, for drizzling and frying

220 g feta cheese

Sift the flour and salt into a bowl, add 2 teaspoons of the olive oil and 150 ml water and mix until it becomes an elastic, neat ball. Transfer to a floured work surface and start stretching and kneading with the palm of your hand for 5 minutes. Cover with clingfilm and leave to rest for at least 30 minutes.

Divide the dough in two and roll out the pieces, one at a time, on a floured surface into a large circle, preferably using a thin rolling pin. Keep turning the dough round and over, sprinkling a little flour, until you have a thin pastry circle of about 60 cm diameter.

Crumble half the cheese all over the circle, sprinkle with 1 tablespoon olive oil and start folding the pie. First roll the two diametrically opposite sides like two fat cigars until they meet at the centre. Now comes the clever bit – holding one end of the pastry down, roll the opposite end round it like a flat snail. You should end up with a tightly coiled pie.

Heat some oil over medium heat in a frying pan big enough to fit the pie. Lift the pie with a flat spatula and slide it into the pan. Fry until light golden on the underside, then turn it over carefully and fry it on the other side. The whole frying operation is swift and it takes about 6–7 minutes. Remove and put on a plate lined with kitchen paper.

Repeat with the remaining pastry and cheese and serve immediately.

Swiss *chard, feta* & *egg* pie

serves 6

 V

'Pide' is a Turkish bread often served alongside colourful and delicious dips. Pide dough is also the base for the Turkish version of pizza, which is often filled or topped with the freshest of vegetables such as tomatoes, spinach or chard, or tangy feta cheese and sometimes with an egg or two cracked on top before being baked. It's very easy to see where the inspiration for this delicious pie came from!

3 tablespoons olive oil

1 red onion, sliced

2 garlic cloves, sliced

500 g Swiss chard, cut into 2-cm pieces

4 eggs

200 g feta cheese, crumbled

salt and black pepper

Pastry

250 g plain flour

150 g unsalted butter, cubed

2 egg yolks

2–3 tablespoons iced water

a large baking tray

To make the pastry, put the flour and butter in the bowl of a food processor and put the bowl in the freezer for 10 minutes.

Pulse the ingredients a few times until just combined. With the motor of the food processor running, add the egg yolks and just enough iced water so that the mixture is on the verge of coming together. Do not overbeat, as this will make the pastry tough. Remove the dough from the bowl and use lightly floured hands to quickly form it into a ball. Wrap in clingfilm and leave to rest in the fridge for 30 minutes.

Put 2 tablespoons of the oil in a frying pan over high heat, add the onion and garlic and cook for 2 minutes, until it softens and just flavours the oil. Add the Swiss chard to the pan and cook for about 5 minutes, stirring often, until it wilts and softens. Season well, leave in the pan and set aside to cool.

Preheat the oven to 220°C (425°F) Gas 7.

Roll the dough out on a sheet of lightly floured greaseproof paper to form a circle about 35 cm in diameter, trimming away any uneven bits. Roll the edge over to form a 1-cm border, then roll over again. Transfer the pastry circle to the large baking tray. Spoon the Swiss chard mixture over the pastry. Crack the eggs in a bowl and prick the yolks with a fork. Pour the eggs over the Swiss chard so that they are evenly distributed, then scatter the feta over the top. Drizzle the remaining oil over the pie and cook in the preheated oven for about 20 minutes, until the pastry is golden and the top of the pie is just starting to turn brown.

Leave to cool for 10 minutes before cutting into slices to serve.

roast chicken with bay leaves

roast *chicken* with *bay leaves*

This is the poor man's version of a dish in which truffle slices are stuffed under the chicken skin.

Preheat the oven to 220°C (425°F) Gas 7.

Season the inside of the chicken and stuff with the lemon quarters, 2 of the bay leaves and the fresh thyme. Separate the skin from the breast meat and put 1 bay leaf on each side of the breast, underneath the skin. Put the remaining 2 bay leaves under the skin of the thighs. Rub the outside of the chicken all over with oil, season and sprinkle over the dried thyme.

Put the chicken on its side on a rack set over a roasting tin. Pour in a 1-cm depth of water and add the sliced lemon and onion. Cook in the preheated oven for 40 minutes, then turn the chicken on its other side. Continue roasting until cooked through and the juices run clear when a thigh is pierced with a skewer, about 40 minutes more. Add extra water to the tin if necessary during cooking. Transfer the chicken from the rack to a plate and leave, covered, for 10 minutes. Add 250 ml water or the wine, if using, to the pan juices and cook over high heat, scraping the bottom of the tin, 3–5 minutes. Stir in the butter. Serve the chicken with the pan juices.

serves **4**

M

1 chicken, about 1.5 kg

2 unwaxed lemons,
1 quartered, 1 sliced

6 large fresh bay leaves

2 sprigs of fresh thyme

1–2 tablespoons olive oil

1 teaspoon dried thyme

1 onion, sliced

250 ml dry white wine
(optional)

1 tablespoon unsalted butter

salt

a roasting tin with a rack

spareribs with *orange* glaze

This is finger food; very messy and not elegant to eat, but perfect for an informal gathering.

Put the marmalade, honey, Worcestershire, soy sauce, lime juice, cayenne, ginger, cumin, oregano and ½ teaspoon salt in a saucepan and stir well. Cook over low heat, stirring often, until the marmalade has melted completely. Set aside until needed.

Preheat the oven to 180°C (350°F) Gas 4.

Brush the ribs lightly with oil and arrange in a roasting tin with the meaty side up. Cook in the preheated oven. Total cooking time is about 2 hours, but turn the ribs every 30 minutes for the first 1½ hours. After this time, baste the ribs with the sauce on both sides. Return to the tin, meat side down. Cook for 15 minutes, baste generously all over again, turn the ribs and cook for about 10 minutes more. Remove from the oven, slice into ribs and serve hot.

serves **4**

M

300 g orange marmalade

325 g honey

4 tablespoons Worcestershire sauce

1 tablespoon soy sauce

juice of 1 lime

1 teaspoon cayenne pepper

1 teaspoon ground ginger

1 teaspoon ground cumin

1 teaspoon dried oregano

salt

1.5 kg spareribs

olive oil, for brushing

slow-cooked spiced *pork belly*

1 tablespoon fennel seeds

2 teaspoons caraway seeds

4 garlic cloves

2 tablespoons olive oil

1 kg pork belly

4 eating apples

2 fennel bulbs, with feathery tops intact, cut into thick wedges

salt and black pepper

serves **4**

M

This is frugal entertaining at its finest. Pork belly is cheap to buy and handsomely rewards patient cooks by producing crispy skin and melt-in-the-mouth meat. It really is the best cut for this dish, but you could also roast a shoulder or leg joint of pork if you wanted. This is one of the best Saturday night dinner recipes – it greets your guests with a delicious aroma, creating a mood of anticipation, which helps to get the evening off to a great start.

Combine the fennel and caraway seeds, garlic and 1 tablespoon salt in a mortar and pound with a pestle. Stir in 1 tablespoon of the olive oil. Cut 5-mm deep incisions, spaced 2 cm apart, across the skin of the pork. Rub the spice mixture into the incisions and leave the pork to sit for 1 hour at cool room temperature.

Preheat the oven to 140°C (275°F) Gas 1.

Put the pork in a large roasting tin and cook in the preheated oven for 3 hours in total. (You'll need to remove the tin from the oven 30 minutes before the end of the cooking time to add the apples and fennel.)

Put the remaining oil in a large bowl and season. Add the apples and the fennel bulbs with feathery tops to the bowl and use your hands to toss until evenly coated in oil. Thirty minutes before the end of the cooking time, remove the pork from the oven and arrange the apples and fennel in the tin. Increase the heat to 220°C (425°F) Gas 7 and return the tin to the oven.

Remove the pork from the oven, cover loosely with foil and leave to rest for about 20 minutes. Carve into slices and serve with the roasted apples and fennel on the side.

roast *pork* with baked *apples*

Get your butcher to score lines in the skin about 2 cm apart: this will produce fantastic crackling, which many people regard as the highlight of roast pork. For the complete Sunday roast, provide some crunchy roast potatoes too.

1.5-kg loin of pork, boned and rolled

3 eating apples

1 onion, chopped

8 fresh sage leaves, chopped

1 tablespoon olive oil

salt and black pepper

Gravy

2 tablespoons plain flour

200 ml white wine

200 ml hot Vegetable Stock (page 54)

Preheat the oven to 220°C (425°F) Gas 7 and lightly oil a roasting tin.

Dry the loin of pork with kitchen paper, place in the prepared tin and roast for 30 minutes. Reduce the heat to 180°C (350°F) Gas 4 and cook the pork for a further 30 minutes.

Slice the apples in half across the middle and cut out the core. Mix the onion and sage with the oil and some seasoning. Arrange the apple halves around the roasting pork and fill the cavities with the stuffing. Return to the oven and cook for 30 minutes. When cooked, transfer the pork and apples to a carving plate and keep warm.

To make the gravy, drain half the fat from the roasting tin, add the flour and mix until smooth. Pour in the wine and stock and mix thoroughly. Place the roasting tin directly over the heat and keep stirring until the gravy thickens. Adjust the seasoning to taste. For a very smooth gravy, press it through a sieve. Serve the pork with the roast apples, the gravy, and roast potatoes, if you like.

pot roast leg of *lamb* with *rosemary* & *onion* gravy

1.5-kg leg of lamb

2 tablespoons olive oil

3 garlic cloves, crushed

2 tablespoons freshly chopped rosemary

3 large fresh rosemary sprigs

2 fresh bay leaves

4 large onions, thinly sliced

300 ml dry white wine

2 teaspoons Dijon mustard

salt and black pepper

serves
6

M

The perfect cook-and-forget roast. The meat is cooked on a bed of rosemary and onions until it is completely tender all the way through – no pink bits – and the onions are melting into the rosemary gravy. Purée the meat juices with the soft onions for a wonderful creamy sauce. Serve with vegetables of your choice.

Preheat the oven to 170°C (325°F) Gas 3.

Trim the lamb of any excess fat. Heat the oil in a lidded, ovenproof casserole dish in which the lamb will fit snugly. Add the lamb and brown it all over. Remove to a plate and leave to cool.

Crush the garlic and chopped rosemary together with a pestle and mortar. Using a small sharp knife, make little incisions all over the lamb. Push the paste well into these incisions. Season well.

Put the rosemary sprigs, bay leaves and onions in the casserole and put the lamb on top. Mix the wine with the mustard, then pour into the casserole. Bring to the boil, cover tightly, then cook in a preheated oven for 1½ hours, turning the lamb over twice.

Raise the oven temperature to 200°C (400°F) Gas 6 and remove the lid from the casserole. Cook for another 30 minutes. The lamb should be very tender and completely cooked through.

Carefully remove the lamb to a serving dish and keep it warm. Skim the fat from the cooking juices and remove the bay leaves and rosemary sprigs. Add a little water if too thick, then bring to the boil, scraping the bottom of the pan to mix in the sediment. Pour the sauce into a blender or food processor and blend until smooth. Season to taste and serve with the lamb.

Yankee pot roast with braised *root vegetables*

The pot roast is one of the great American classics – and when it appears with braised vegetables, it becomes Yankee Pot Roast. It's made with silverside, which is an inexpensive cut of beef, and when served with these root vegetables, it really is an ideal option for a tasty and filling, budget family lunch. Bear in mind that the meat needs to marinate for at least 3 hours (or even overnight) before cooking.

serves
4

M

1 kg rolled silverside

3 tablespoons olive oil

1 tablespoon ground allspice

2 tablespoons plain flour

1 tablespoon mustard powder

150 ml red wine

500 ml hot Beef Stock (page 53)

6 tablespoons butter

4 parsnips, cut into 5-cm pieces

2 sweet potatoes, cut into 5-cm pieces

2 carrots, cut into 5-cm pieces

12 small red onions, cut into 4 wedges through the root

2 tablespoons cornflour

salt and black pepper

Put the silverside in a shallow dish. Put 1 tablespoon of the olive oil, the allspice, 1 teaspoon salt, the flour and mustard in a small bowl and mix to form a paste, adding more oil as necessary. Rub the silverside with the mixture, cover and marinate in the refrigerator for 3 hours or overnight.

Preheat the oven to 180°C (350°F) Gas 4.

Remove the meat and shake off any excess spices. Heat the remaining oil in a large frying pan, add the meat and brown on all sides. Transfer to a lidded, ovenproof casserole dish.

Add the wine to the frying pan, bring to the boil and cook until reduced by two-thirds. Add the stock and bring to the boil, pour over the meat, cover with a lid and cook in the preheated oven for 1½ hours, or until tender.

Add the butter to the frying pan, heat gently, then add the vegetables and fry until they take on a little colour. Season, cover with a lid and simmer in their own juices for 20 minutes. Keep them warm.

When the meat is cooked, drain off the liquid into a saucepan. Mix the cornflour with 3 tablespoons water and blend it into the liquid. Bring to the boil, then taste and adjust the seasoning. Pour the sauce back over the meat and vegetables and heat on top of the stove.

To serve, transfer the meat to a platter and arrange the reheated vegetables around. Serve the gravy separately.

Thai-style *fish* with *tomato* relish

3 ripe tomatoes

2 large red chillies

1 whole garlic bulb, unpeeled

6 shallots, unpeeled

1 tablespoon lemon juice

2 tablespoons Thai fish sauce

4 long stalks of fresh coriander, with roots intact

4 garlic cloves, chopped

½ teaspoon black peppercorns

4 x 200-g white fish fillets, such as cod, hake or haddock

lime halves, for squeezing

a baking tray, lined with greaseproof paper

serves
4

F

This is an authentic Thai treat you can easily replicate at home. The tasty tomato relish is also great served with grilled chicken or gently heated and stirred through some cooked prawns.

Preheat the oven to 220°C (425°F) Gas 7.

Put the tomatoes, chillies, garlic bulb and shallots in a roasting tin and cook in the preheated oven for 10–15 minutes. Remove the tin from the oven, transfer the chillies, garlic and shallots to a bowl and cover. (This will make them sweat and therefore be easier to peel.) Return the tomatoes to the oven for a further 5 minutes, then add them to the bowl with the other vegetables and cover.

When cool enough to handle, peel the tomatoes and chillies and put the flesh in a food processor. Squeeze the soft flesh of the shallots and garlic out of their skins and add. Blend to make a chunky sauce. Stir in the lemon juice and 1 tablespoon of the fish sauce and set aside.

Reduce the oven temperature to 180°C (350°F) Gas 4.

Cut off the coriander roots, clean and roughly chop. Reserve a few leaves to garnish and chop the remaining leaves and stalks. Put the roots in a mortar with the garlic cloves, peppercorns and remaining fish sauce and pound with a pestle to make a paste.

Put the fish fillets on the prepared baking tray. Spread a quarter of the coriander paste over each fillet. Cook in the preheated oven for 20 minutes. Serve with the relish spooned over the top and lime halves on the side for squeezing. Garnish with the reserved coriander leaves.

sardines baked with garlic, lemon, olive oil & breadcrumbs

When opened up and boned, sardines cook in minutes in a hot oven. Marinating them in oil and lemon juice lends piquancy to the delicate flesh. This is a good dish to prepare a day ahead, then serve for lunch with salad.

serves
4

F

8 whole sardines, cleaned

100 ml olive oil

finely grated zest and juice of
1 unwaxed lemon

2 garlic cloves, thinly sliced

3 tablespoons freshly
chopped flat leaf parsley

1 tablespoon salted capers,
drained and chopped

3 tablespoons breadcrumbs

salt and black pepper

lemon wedges, to serve

Preheat the oven to 200°C (400°F) Gas 6.

Make sure the sardines have been scaled. If not, scale them with the blunt edge of a knife. Cut off the heads and slit open the bellies. Remove the guts under running water if they haven't already been removed. Slide your thumb along the backbone to release the flesh along its length. Take hold of the backbone at the head end and lift it out. The fish should now be open flat like a book.

Put the oil, lemon zest and juice in a large bowl, whisk well, then stir in the garlic, parsley, capers and some seasoning. Holding each sardine by the tail, dip in the lemony olive oil, then put skin side up in a baking dish. Pour in any remaining liquid, sprinkle with the breadcrumbs and bake in the preheated oven for 15 minutes.

Serve warm immediately, or leave to cool, then store overnight in the refrigerator. Serve the next day at room temperature, when the sardines will have marinated in the oil, lemon and herbs. Serve with the lemon wedges.

desserts

ginger & caramel oranges

150 g granulated sugar

3 cm fresh ginger, peeled and sliced

140 ml double cream

15 g unsalted butter

5 oranges

2 balls of preserved ginger in syrup, drained and diced

serves **4**

Q

V

It takes a while to get the hang of properly peeling oranges so they are pith-free but it's worth the effort. The fruit you end up with is refreshing and sharp, which is why it contrasts so well with the sticky, sweet caramel. The preserved ginger warms up the dish and complements the orange beautifully.

Put the sugar, 75 ml water and the fresh ginger in a saucepan over low heat and heat gently until the sugar has dissolved. Turn up the heat and boil until the edges start to turn golden. Without stirring the syrup, swirl the pan until the syrup is an even teak colour. Pour in another 75 ml water and the double cream to thin the syrup down to a runny caramel. Add the butter and set aside to cool slightly.

Cut the tops and bases off the oranges so they stand flat on a chopping board. Using a small, serrated knife, cut off the skin and pith, following the curve of the orange, all the way round until you have taken off all the pith. Slice the remaining orange flesh thinly.

Transfer the oranges to bowls, scatter with the preserved ginger and drizzle with the caramel.

rhubarb compote with yoghurt

500 g rhubarb, trimmed

50 g caster sugar, or to taste

125 g natural yoghurt

1 tablespoon clear honey

½ tablespoon rosewater

serves **4**

V

Rosewater, like orange flower water, is sold in the baking section of supermarkets, in chemist shops, and in ethnic food stores specializing in Middle Eastern or Indian products. Make this to have for a refreshing dessert, or for breakfast.

Cut the rhubarb into 5-cm slices and put into a saucepan. Add the sugar and 4 tablespoons water. Bring to the boil, cover and simmer gently for 15 minutes until the rhubarb has softened. Taste and stir in a little extra sugar if necessary. Transfer to a dish and leave to cool.

Put the yoghurt, honey and rosewater into a bowl, mix well, then serve with the rhubarb.

ginger & caramel oranges

toasted oat yoghurt & red berries

toasted *oat yoghurt* & *red berries*

Baking the oats adds a caramel crunch to this simple pudding. If you don't have the berries, use whatever fruit you have already – bananas, apples, pears or peaches are all good.

 serves 4

 V

Preheat the grill.

Put the rolled oats and sugar into a bowl and mix. Sprinkle evenly over the prepared baking tray and put under the hot grill. Toast until golden and caramelized, then remove and leave to cool on the tray.

Put half the berries into a bowl and coarsely crush with the back of a spoon. Add the yoghurt and toasted oats and mix lightly until marbled. Spoon into 4 glasses and top with the remaining berries and the honey. Chill until ready to serve.

50 g rolled oats

20 g light brown soft sugar

300 g mixed berries

200 ml Greek yoghurt

4 tablespoons clear honey

a baking tray, lined with greaseproof paper

iced *summer berries* with hot *white chocolate* sauce

175 g white chocolate, chopped

150 ml single cream

1 teaspoon lavender honey

450 g frozen mixed summer berries (such as blueberries, strawberries, raspberries, blackberries and redcurrants)

serves
4

Q

V

This is the ultimate in simple puddings – if you have these ingredients in your fridge, freezer and storecupboard, you will never be caught out by unexpected guests. The secret is to make sure that the summer fruits are just frozen before pouring over the hot white chocolate sauce.

Remove the summer berries from the freezer 10 minutes before you want to serve them.

Put the white chocolate, cream and honey in a heatproof bowl and set over a pan of simmering water. Do not let the base of the bowl touch the water. Stir continuously with a rubber or wooden spatula, until the chocolate has melted and you have a smooth sauce. Alternatively, you can melt the chocolate with the cream and honey in the microwave. Be careful because white chocolate scorches easily, so don't overcook it.

Arrange the semi-frozen berries on individual serving plates, then pour the hot white chocolate sauce all over the berries so that the heat of the sauce begins to melt and soften them. Serve immediately.

strawberries with *black pepper*

500 g strawberries

1 tablespoon orange flower water (optional)

1 tablespoon caster sugar

2 teaspoons cracked black pepper

serves
4

Q

V

Strawberries and black pepper are surprisingly good partners. The orange flower water adds a lovely perfumed quality to the strawberries, but can be omitted.

Hull the strawberries and cut in half. Sprinkle with the orange flower water, if using, and with the sugar and black pepper. Chill for 15 minutes.

Note: Strawberries should be washed and dried before hulling, not after, otherwise they fill up with water.

iced summer berries with
hot white chocolate sauce

berry gratin

The sweet and frothy egg mixture spread on top of the fruit is called a sabayon, making this a very easy and elegant dessert. Use whatever berries are ripe, in season and in abundance, or frozen berries if you like. The gratin is best when made with a bit of something alcoholic. The recipe requires only a small amount of wine and the remainder is just the thing to drink with this dish – ideal for special occasions.

serves
4

600 g frozen mixed berries, thawed, or 400 g fresh

5 large egg yolks and 3 egg whites

80 g caster sugar

1 tablespoon clear honey

125 ml sweet dessert wine (optional)

1–2 tablespoons icing sugar

4 shallow, ovenproof gratin dishes

Preheat the grill to high and divide the fruit between the gratin dishes.

Bring a saucepan of water just to simmering point. Choose a heatproof bowl (glass is ideal) that will sit tightly on top of the saucepan. Put the egg yolks and sugar in the bowl and whisk, off the heat, until blended. Transfer the bowl to the saucepan and continue whisking, over the heat, until the mixture is thick and frothy, 2–4 minutes. Don't let the water boil. Whisk in the honey and wine if using, and remove from the heat.

Beat the egg whites in another bowl until they hold stiff peaks.

Gently fold the beaten whites into the warm yolk mixture until blended. Divide between the gratin dishes, spreading evenly to cover the fruit. Lightly sprinkle the top of each with a dusting of icing sugar (this will help it to colour nicely). Cook under the hot grill until just browned, 1–2 minutes (watch carefully because they will colour quite quickly). Serve immediately.

Note: To use up the egg whites left over after making this recipe, see recipes on pages 211, 227 and 233.

banana fritters

2 large bananas

cinnamon ice cream, to serve (optional)

Ginger batter

40 g plain flour

a pinch of salt

1 egg, separated

75 ml ginger beer or sparkling water

1 tablespoon sunflower oil, plus extra for deep-frying

serves
4

Q

V

Fruit fritters are delicious and very simple to make. They take no time at all to prepare so even if you haven't planned to have dessert, you can probably rustle this up without too much bother – in fact it's a useful sweet recipe for unexpected guests. Cinnamon and banana make an excellent flavour combination, so serve these with cinnamon ice cream, if you can find it. You can also use this batter to make apple or pineapple fritters. Make sure you have enough sunflower oil before you start – you will need quite a large amount for the deep-frying.

Preheat the oven to a very low setting.

Peel the bananas, cut into 4 chunks, then cut the chunks in half lengthways.

To make the batter, sift the flour and salt into a bowl, beat in the egg yolk, ginger beer or sparkling water and oil to form a smooth batter. Whisk the egg white in a separate bowl until soft peaks form, then fold into the batter.

Heat 5 cm sunflower oil in deep saucepan until it reaches 180°C (350°F) or until a cube of bread turns golden brown in 30 seconds.

Dip the banana chunks into the batter and deep-fry in batches of 3–4 for about 1 minute until the batter is crisp and golden. Drain on kitchen paper and keep them warm in a moderate oven while you cook the remainder. Serve with a scoop of cinnamon ice cream, if you like.

sticky fried *bananas* on *toast*

One mouthful of these buttery, sticky, gooey, tangy bananas will transport you to another world – just be careful about putting too much in your mouth in one go because those bananas are HOT when they first come out of the pan! Challah, the delicious, dense Jewish bread, makes the perfect base, but any good-quality white bread will be divine.

Melt the butter in a non-stick pan until sizzling, then add the bananas and fry for about 2 minutes. Turn them over, sprinkle with the brown sugar and continue cooking for a further 2–3 minutes, gently nudging the bananas around the pan, but take care not to break them up.

Add the brandy and cook for 1 minute more until the bananas are soft and tender, letting the juices bubble. Remove the pan from the heat, squeeze over the lime juice and jiggle the bananas to mix.

Meanwhile, lightly toast the bread on both sides, add the bananas and top with a generous scoop of vanilla ice cream. Serve immediately.

serves
2

50 g unsalted butter, plus extra for spreading

3 perfectly ripe bananas, sliced

2 tablespoons brown sugar

1 tablespoon brandy

½ lime

2 thick slices of challah or white bread

vanilla ice cream, to serve

sticky fried bananas on toast

crêpes

In France, crêpes are either street food (as in Paris), a cheap meal for students (from a crêperie), or something made on Sunday evening as a light meal after the long and laden Sunday lunch. However you look at them, they are the most wonderfully versatile base for all things sweet, sticky and molten (and savoury too, of course). The choice of filling is entirely up to you and the contents of your storecupboard.

250 g plain flour

3 large eggs, beaten

500 ml whole milk

2 tablespoons sugar

unsalted butter, for cooking

Put the flour in a large bowl and make a hollow in the middle. Pour the eggs into the hollow. Using a wooden spoon, gradually beat the eggs into the flour. Stir well because you don't want too many lumps. Pour the milk in slowly, stirring constantly, until completely blended. Stir in the sugar. Leave to stand for at least 1 hour.

Heat a small, non-stick frying pan over medium heat. Add a lump of butter, melt and swirl to coat. Add a ladle of batter to the pan and swirl to spread thinly but evenly. Cook until browning around the edges and bubbly in the middle, then flip over and cook for a few minutes longer.

As a rule, the first few crêpes are not perfect because it takes a while for the pan to get to just the right temperature, and for the cook to get warmed up. Continue cooking until all the batter is used up, occasionally adding more butter as needed. Serve warm, with the filling of your choice.

Fillings

• A lump of butter run over the hot crêpe, followed by a sprinkling of caster sugar, then a generous squeeze of lemon juice. Liqueur is also a nice alternative to the lemon juice – try Grand Marnier.

• Try chocolate sauce, jam, thinly sliced apples sautéed in butter, sweetened chestnut purée and crème fraîche, orange flower or rose water, or honey.

• Ice cream and/or whipped cream, optionally sprinkled with chopped nuts, sliced bananas and/or strawberries.

Norwegian *apple* bake

2 eggs

250 g unrefined caster sugar

100 g unsalted butter

150 ml milk

4 cooking apples, cored, peeled and sliced

175 g self-raising flour

½ teaspoon grated nutmeg

thick cream or vanilla ice cream, to serve

a shallow baking dish, 30 cm in diameter, greased

serves
4

This is such a good standby pudding – usually, you will have all the dry ingredients in your cupboard. You can use any kind of apples, pears or even plums.

Preheat the oven to 180°C (350°F) Gas 5.

Put the eggs into a large bowl, add 200 g of the sugar and whisk until stiff and creamy. Put the butter and milk into a saucepan and heat gently until the butter has melted. Meanwhile, arrange the apple slices in the prepared baking dish.

Gradually add the hot milk and butter to the egg mixture, whisking well. Fold in the flour to make a smooth batter. Pour the mixture over the apples, then sprinkle with the remaining sugar and the nutmeg. Bake in the preheated oven for 20–25 minutes, or until puffed and golden. Serve hot or cold with scoops of thick cream or vanilla ice cream.

Polish cheesecake with *berries*

75 g unsalted butter, softened

200 g caster sugar

3 eggs, separated

1 teaspoon vanilla extract

750 g cream cheese

2 teaspoons cornflour

1 teaspoon baking powder

a selection of summer berries, to serve

a Swiss roll tin, 33 x 23 cm, greased and lined with greaseproof paper

serves
6

This rich, dense, but surprisingly light cheesecake is served in shallow slices. It works equally well served with a strong espresso or as a pudding at the end of a meal.

Preheat the oven to 150°C (300°F) Gas 2.

Put the butter, sugar, egg yolks and vanilla in a bowl. Whisk with an electric beater until the mixture is pale and creamy.

Put the egg whites in a clean, dry bowl and whisk until soft peaks form.

Using a metal spoon, very lightly stir the cream cheese, cornflour and baking powder into the butter mixture. Add the egg whites and mix lightly. Spoon into the prepared Swiss roll tin and spread evenly with a spatula. Bake in the preheated oven for 1 hour. Remove from the oven and leave to cool in the tin. Cut the cheesecake into 12 portions and gently ease away from the greaseproof paper. Very carefully remove the slices of cheesecake, taking care not to break them. Serve 2 slices per person, with the berries.

Norwegian apple bake

piña colada sherbet

piña colada sherbet

This is a cross between an ice cream and a sorbet. It makes a fantastically refreshing end to the meal.

serves
6–8

V

Put the sugar in a pan with 200 ml water over very low heat, stirring occasionally, until the sugar has dissolved. Bring to the boil without stirring and boil for about 4 minutes. Set aside to cool.

Put the pineapple in a food processor and process to a juice. Strain through a sieve. This should give you about 550–600 ml juice. Mix in the coconut cream, cooled sugar syrup, lime juice and rum, which should give you just over 1 litre liquid.

Cover, transfer the sherbet mixture to the fridge and chill for a couple of hours. Pour into an ice-cream machine and churn, adding the egg whites halfway through. (You may need to do this in 2 batches). If you haven't got an ice-cream machine, pour the sherbet mix into a lidded plastic box and freeze for about 1½ hours or until beginning to harden at the edges. Put the egg whites in a food processor, process briefly until frothy, then tip in the half-frozen sherbet mixture and whizz until smooth. Return the sherbet mix to the freezer, freeze for another hour, then whizz again.

Freeze and whizz a third time for extra smoothness. Leave to harden. Before serving, remove the sherbet from the freezer and leave to mellow in the fridge for about 20 minutes. Serve with a selection of tropical fruits.

Note: To use up the egg yolks left over after making this recipe, see recipes on pages 203, 219, 229, 233 and 234.

150 g unrefined caster sugar

1 ripe pineapple, peeled, cored and cubed

200 ml coconut cream

6 tablespoons lime juice (from 2–3 limes)

4 tablespoons white rum

2 large egg whites, beaten

an ice-cream machine (optional)

iced lemon crush

This is a light and cleansing end to a summer's lunch, with all the sunshine flavour of lemons.

serves
4

V

Put the zest and sugar in a saucepan with 250 ml cold water and bring to the boil for 5 minutes. Strain. Add 500 ml cold water and the lemon juice, pour into a freezerproof container and freeze for about 1 hour until ice crystals have formed around the edge. Break up with a fork and serve. Add extra crushed ice, if using.

coarsely grated zest and juice of 8 unwaxed lemons

200 g caster sugar

extra crushed ice (optional)

plum crumble

8–10 ripe plums

4–5 tablespoons sugar

pouring cream, to serve

Crumble topping

75 g unsalted butter,
chilled and cubed

175 g plain flour

a pinch of salt

50 g caster sugar

*a medium, shallow baking
dish*

 serves **4–6**

 V

Plums have such a rich flavour when they are cooked that they need little or no other flavourings with them, except perhaps a pinch of cinnamon. Use the ripest plums you can find. This is a great favourite with children.

Preheat the oven to 180°C (350°F) Gas 4 and put a baking tray on the middle shelf to heat up.

Halve the plums and remove the stones. Cut the halves into quarters if they are very large. Toss them with the sugar and tip them into the baking dish.

To make the crumble topping, rub the butter into the flour with the salt until it resembles rough breadcrumbs. Stir in the sugar. Lightly scatter the topping mixture over the plums. Place the baking dish on the baking tray in the preheated oven and bake for 40–45 minutes, until golden brown. Remove from the oven and serve warm with pouring cream.

blackberry crumble

375 g blackberries
(about 2 punnets)

1 tablespoon caster sugar

1 teaspoon cornflour

Crumble topping

75 g unsalted butter,
chilled and cubed

130 g plain flour

60 g light brown soft sugar

double cream, to serve

*a medium, shallow baking
dish*

serves **4**

V

After a long walk and a successful session of blackberry-picking, why not bake this simple crumble, which will bring out the best in your delicious fresh blackberries.

Preheat the oven to 180°C (350°F) Gas 4.

Put the blackberries in a bowl with the caster sugar and the cornflour and toss to mix. Tumble the berries into the baking dish and set aside for 15–20 minutes.

To make the crumble topping, rub the butter into the flour until it resembles rough breadcrumbs. Stir in the sugar. Lightly scatter the topping mixture over the berries and bake in the preheated oven for 45–50 minutes, until the top is golden brown. Leave the crumble to cool slightly before serving with dollops of cream spooned on top.

plum crumble

mulled *winter fruit* crumble

Christmas is definitely coming when the smell of this crumble
starts to drift around the house. A mixture of traditionally
festive dried fruits provides a rich base for the light crumble
topping. The spicy mulled wine seeps into the fruits as they
cook and plumps them up nicely. This is a lovely alternative
to mince pies!

serves
4

V

Preheat the oven to 190°C (375°F) Gas 5 and put a baking tray on the middle
shelf to heat up.

Chop the dried fruits into bite-sized pieces and place in a non-reactive
saucepan. Add the wine, mulling spices, orange zest and caster sugar. Heat
gently, then simmer for 10 minutes. Set aside to cool.

Spoon the semi-cooked dried fruit into the baking dish and remove the
mulling spices and orange zest.

To make the crumble topping, rub the butter into the flour, mixed spice and
salt until it resembles rough breadcrumbs. Stir in the sugar. (At this stage
you can pop it into a plastic bag and chill in the fridge until needed.)

Lightly scatter the topping mixture over the dried fruits, mounding it up a
little towards the centre. Place on top of the baking tray in the preheated
oven and bake for about 25 minutes, or until crisp and golden on top.
Remove from the oven and leave to cool for 5 minutes before serving with
clotted cream.

350 g mixed dried fruits
(such as apples, apricots,
figs, raisins, cranberries)

300 ml red wine

1 small muslin bag of mulled
wine spices (cinnamon,
cloves, allspice)

a strip of orange zest

50 g caster sugar

clotted cream, to serve

Spiced topping

100 g unsalted butter,
chilled and cubed

200 g wholemeal flour

¼ teaspoon mixed spice

a pinch of salt

100 g demerera sugar

a medium, shallow baking
dish

225 g plain flour

¼ teaspoon mixed spice (optional)

150 g caster sugar

a large pinch of salt

4 teaspoons baking powder

250 ml milk

½ teaspoon vanilla extract

50 g unsalted butter

675 g fresh or frozen blackberries

a large, shallow, metal baking tin

blackberry cobbler

serves
4–6

V

This is an American version of French clafoutis, but without the eggs. The batter uses more flour and has baking powder instead of eggs to lift it.

Preheat the oven to 180°C (350°F) Gas 4.

Sift the flour, spice (if using) sugar, salt and baking powder into a bowl. Gradually whisk in the milk and vanilla to give a thick batter. Leave to stand for 15 minutes.

Melt the butter over gentle heat in the metal baking tin. Give the rested batter a quick stir, then pour the batter into the tin over the melted butter. Don't worry if the butter floats around and mingles with the batter at this stage. Immediately scatter the blackberries over the batter and bake in the preheated oven for about 55 minutes, or until the batter is puffed and set around the blackberries. Remove from the oven and serve warm.

500 g rhubarb, chopped

5 cm fresh ginger, peeled and grated

2 tablespoons caster sugar

7 bananas, thickly cut diagonally

¼ teaspoon ground cinnamon

Oat topping

90 g unsalted butter, chilled and cubed

125 g plain flour

125 g demerara sugar

50 g rolled oats

a pie dish, 25 cm in diameter, lightly greased

rhubarb, ginger & *banana* crumble

serves
4

V

This is a crumble with a banana twist, making a wicked combination with rhubarb, ginger and crunchy oats in the crumble topping. It's a winning pudding.

Preheat the oven to 200°C (400°F) Gas 6.

Put the rhubarb in a saucepan and add the ginger, sugar and 2 tablespoons water. Bring to the boil and simmer for 7–10 minutes, until the rhubarb has softened. Transfer to a blender and process to a purée. Transfer to the prepared pie dish and top with the bananas and a sprinkling of cinnamon.

To make the crumble topping, rub the butter into the flour until it resembles rough breadcrumbs. Stir in the sugar and two-thirds of the oats. Lightly scatter the topping over the fruit mixture and top with the remaining oats. Bake in the preheated oven for 30–40 minutes.

blackberry cobbler

blackberry & *apple* pie

For the best pastry results, always use a metal pie dish: it will get hotter than ceramic and guarantees to cook the pastry until dry and crumbly rather than soggy. If you're lucky enough to have an apple tree in the garden (or to know someone who does), keep this recipe handy for when there is a glut of fallen apples to use up and a horde of hungry mouths to feed.

serves
4–6

V

Put the flour and butter into a food processor and process until the mixture looks like breadcrumbs. Add the sugar and process briefly. With the machine running, gradually add 3 egg yolks until the mixture comes together to form a ball. (You can add the extra egg yolk if it is too dry.) Transfer the pastry to a lightly floured surface and knead very gently with your hands until smooth. Divide in half, wrap each piece in clingfilm and chill for 40 minutes.

Preheat the oven to 220°C (425°F) Gas 7.

Remove 1 piece of chilled pastry from the fridge and roll out until just larger than the pie dish. Put the rolled pastry into the pie dish, pressing the base and rim gently to push out any air bubbles. Layer the apple slices, blackberries and sugar over the pastry, piling the fruit high, then brush milk over the pastry rim.

Roll out the remaining pastry to just bigger than the dish and drape it over the fruit, taking care not to stretch it. Trim the excess pastry away from the edge and then go around the rim of the pie, pinching the pastry together with your fingers to seal. Using a small, sharp knife, cut a vent in the middle of the pie to let the steam escape.

Brush the pastry all over with milk and sprinkle generously with sugar. Bake in the preheated oven for 30 minutes, then reduce the oven temperature to 180°C (350°F) Gas 4 and bake for another 30 minutes until golden.

350 g plain flour

200 g unsalted butter, chilled and cubed

80 g unrefined caster sugar, plus extra for sprinkling

3–4 egg yolks

milk, for brushing

Filling

800 g cooking apples, such as Bramley, cored, peeled and sliced

400 g blackberries

100 g unrefined caster sugar

a metal pie dish, 25 cm in diameter, lightly greased

cranberry & orange streusel crisp

serves 4

V

500 g fresh or frozen cranberries

finely grated zest and juice of 1 orange

honey, to taste

Streusel topping

75 g plain flour

75 g light brown soft sugar

75 g unsalted butter, chilled and cubed

a small, shallow baking dish

This is really nice made in individual dishes or cups, but make sure they are ovenproof. You can use fresh or frozen cranberries depending on what is most convenient.

Preheat the oven to 220°C (425°F) Gas 7.

Put the cranberries in a saucepan with the orange juice (not the zest) and bring to the boil. Cook for 2 minutes then remove from the heat and sweeten to taste with honey. Pour into the baking dish and leave to cool.

Mix the flour, sugar and orange zest in a bowl and add the butter. Rub the butter into the dry mixture until it resembles fine breadcrumbs and is on no account greasy or oily. Pop into a plastic bag and chill for 20 minutes if it has become so. Once the cranberries are cold, sprinkle evenly with the topping and bake in the preheated oven for 10 minutes, then turn down the oven temperature to 180°C (350°F) Gas 4 and bake for a further 15 minutes.

buttered apricot betty

serves 4

V

675 g fresh apricots or 3 x 400-g tins of apricots in natural juice (not syrup)

100 g unsalted butter, diced

150 g breadcrumbs, lightly toasted

2 tablespoons golden syrup

100 ml orange juice

50 g caster sugar

a medium, deep pie or soufflé dish, greased

This is a very easy-going kind of pudding. Use fresh apricots if you have them, especially if they're going soft, or tinned apricots in their natural juice if that's easier.

Preheat the oven to 190°C (375°F) Gas 5 .

Halve the fresh apricots and flip out the stones. Or drain the tinned apricots and pat dry. Place a layer of apricots on the base of the baking dish. Reserve 4–6 tablespoons of breadcrumbs for the top. Sprinkle some of the rest of the breadcrumbs over the apricots, and dot with some of the butter. Put in some more apricots and repeat these alternate casual layers until all the apricots and breadcrumbs are used up. Use the reserved breadcrumbs for the final top layer.

Warm the syrup with the orange juice, and pour this over the top. Sprinkle with sugar and dot with the remaining butter. Place the pie dish in a roasting tin and pour in enough boiling water to come halfway up the sides of the dish. Bake in the preheated oven for 45 minutes, or until the apricots are soft and the top crispy and brown. Serve warm.

cranberry &
orange streusel crisp

baked lemon pudding

baked *lemon* pudding

This is an old family favourite and perfect for when lemons are in abundance and inexpensive at your local market.

serves
6

V

Preheat the oven to 180°C (350°F) Gas 4.

Put the butter and sugar in a food processor and process for 10 seconds, until smooth. Add the egg yolks one at a time to the mixture and process for a few seconds after each addition. Add the flour and process until smooth. With the motor running pour in the milk in a slow and steady stream, scraping down the bowl of the food processer with a spatula so all the mixture is incorporated and lump free. Transfer the mixture to a large bowl.

Using an electric whisk, beat the egg whites until firm, then fold them into the batter in two batches using a large metal spoon. Quickly stir in the lemon juice. Spoon the mixture into the baking dish and bake in the preheated oven for 25–30 minutes, until golden on top. Leave to rest for 10 minutes before dusting with icing sugar to serve.

50 g unsalted butter

285 g caster sugar

3 eggs, separated

3 tablespoons self-raising flour

375 ml whole milk

65 ml lemon juice

1 tablespoon icing sugar

a medium baking dish

basic *croissant* pudding

Really, this is bread and butter pudding, that old classic devised as a way to use up stale bread, but sometimes, after weekend guests, there are stale croissants to use up. Because the ingredients are always to hand, this is an easy, last-minute pudding option. Use chocolate croissants or brioche, even panettone, if you like. Or embellish the base recipe with chocolate chips, rum-soaked raisins or strawberry or peach conserves spooned on the croissants before adding the custard. Or simply drizzle a bit of maple syrup over the top.

serves
4

V

Preheat the oven to 180°C (350°F) Gas 4.

Cut each croissant into 3 and arrange in the dish. Put the eggs in a mixing bowl and beat well.

Put the milk, crème fraîche and sugar in a measuring jug and whisk well. Pour into the eggs and whisk again, then pour over the croissants. Sprinkle the top liberally with sugar and bake in the preheated oven until golden and the batter is just set, 30–40 minutes. Serve warm.

4 all-butter croissants, preferably stale (not too stale)

3 large eggs

300 ml whole milk

3 heaped tablespoons crème fraîche or double cream

50 g caster sugar, plus extra for sprinkling

2-litre soufflé dish, well greased

flourless *chocolate* cake

200 g dark chocolate, broken in pieces

175 g unsalted butter, chopped

5 large eggs, separated

140 g caster sugar

raspberries, to serve (optional)

cream (double, whipped or crème fraîche)

a non-stick springform cake tin, 24 cm in diameter

serves
6–8

V

Chocolate, butter, eggs and sugar; who needs flour? This is child's play to make and is best when made in advance – ideal for entertaining. It's supposed to be crumbly and almost raw in the middle, so if you're nervous about baking in public, this is the pudding for you because it always looks good. It is also the perfect after-dinner cake, rich and satisfying, and a nice companion when lingering over coffee after dinner.

Preheat the oven to 180°C (350°F) Gas 4.

Put the chocolate and butter in a heatproof bowl set over a pan of simmering water. Do not let the base of the bowl touch the water. Leave to melt, stirring occasionally. Set aside.

Put the egg yolks and all but 2 tablespoons of the sugar in a large bowl. Beat on high until pale and fluffy, about 5 minutes. Set aside.

Put the egg whites in another bowl and beat on high until firm. Add the remaining 2 tablespoons sugar and continue beating until stiff peaks form. Set aside.

Stir the chocolate mixture into the egg yolk mixture and blend well. Add a third of the beaten whites and mix well until there are no white streaks. Carefully fold in the remaining whites, using a rubber spatula, until there are no white streaks. Pour into the cake tin and set it on a baking tray (in case of drips).

Bake in the preheated oven until crisp around the edges, but still jiggly and almost raw looking in the very middle, about 20–30 minutes. Leave to cool slightly, then run a knife around the inside edge of the tin to loosen and remove the outer ring. Serve at room temperature with raspberries, if using, and any kind of cream.

baked *brioche* pudding

serves 6

This is an impressive pudding for relatively little work. The sweet and buttery brioche works well with tangy blackberries.

Preheat the oven to 180°C (350°F) Gas 4.

Slice the brioche to give you 6–8 thin slices. Lightly butter the slices on one side and arrange them in the bottom of the baking dish, overlapping them slightly. Put half the blackberries on top. Repeat with the remaining brioche slices and blackberries. Put the cream, eggs, milk and caster sugar in a bowl or jug and beat to combine. Pour the mixture over the brioche in the baking dish. Cover with foil and leave to sit for 30 minutes to allow the brioche to absorb the liquid.

Sprinkle the raw sugar over the top of the pudding and bake in the preheated oven for 40–45 minutes, or until the top of the pudding is golden.

4 brioche rolls or 200 g brioche loaf

50 g unsalted butter, softened

300 g blackberries

3 eggs

125 ml single cream

375 ml whole milk

75 g caster sugar

2 tablespoons unrefined caster sugar

a medium baking dish

steamed *syrup* pudding

An easy-to-make winter classic, this pudding is always a winner. You could omit the syrup and use the same volume of honey, jam, lemon curd or a little chopped stem ginger.

Put the butter and sugar in a mixing bowl and beat with a wooden spoon until pale and creamy. Add the eggs one at a time and beat until blended. Sift the flour over the egg mixture and fold in. Add the milk and continue folding the mixture until smooth.

Pour the golden syrup into the pudding basin. Spoon the sponge mixture on top. Cover with greaseproof paper and secure with kitchen string.

Sit the pudding basin in a large saucepan. Pour in boiling water from the kettle until it comes about halfway up the sides of the basin. Cover and simmer gently for 1 hour, topping up with more boiling water as necessary.

Carefully remove the pudding basin from the saucepan and peel off the paper. Place a large plate on top of the basin, then turn the pudding over, giving it a gentle shake to release it from the mould. Serve with ice cream.

250 g unsalted butter, softened

250 g caster sugar

3 eggs

375 g self-raising flour

50 ml whole milk

4 tablespoons golden syrup

vanilla ice cream, to serve

a 1-litre pudding basin, greased

brown sugar meringues

baked brioche pudding

brown sugar meringues

Make these ahead, keep in airtight tin, then sandwich together with cream – handy for last-minute puddings. They're also perfect for using up any egg whites you have left over from another recipe.

Preheat the oven to 110°C (225°F) Gas ¼.

Put the egg whites in a large bowl and whisk until very stiff but not dry. Mix the caster sugar and brown sugar, then gradually whisk in the combined sugars, spoonful by spoonful, letting the mixture become very stiff between each addition. Spoon 12 large meringues onto the greaseproof paper. Bake in the preheated oven for 3–4 hours until thoroughly dried out.

Remove the meringues from the oven and leave to cool on the paper. Carefully lift off when cool and store in an airtight container until required.

Note: To use up the egg yolks left over after making this recipe, see recipes on pages 203, 219, 229, 233 and 234.

makes
12

V

4 egg whites

125 g caster sugar

125 g light brown soft sugar

a baking tray, lined with greaseproof paper

buttery jam tarts

buttery *jam* tarts

If you don't have petit four tins, break off pieces of dough, push a finger into the centre for the jam and bake on baking trays.

makes
18

V

Put the flour and cornflour in a large bowl. Rub in the butter until the mixture resembles fine breadcrumbs. Stir in the icing sugar until evenly mixed. Add the egg yolks and bring the mixture together to form a smooth dough. If it is a little sticky, dust with the tiniest bit of flour. Break off pieces the size of walnuts and push them into the tart tin holes. Use a tart tamper, if you have one, to mould the pastry into the tin, otherwise use a finger. Spoon the jam into the centre of each tart. Chill for 30 minutes before baking.

Preheat the oven to 180°C (350°F) Gas 4.

Bake the tarts in the preheated oven for about 10 minutes, until pale golden. Remove from the oven and leave to cool in the tin before turning out.

200 g plain flour

50 g cornflour

100 g unsalted butter, chilled and cubed

120 g icing sugar

2 egg yolks

4–5 tablespoons apricot or strawberry jam

2 x 12-hole petit four-sized tart tins or 2 baking trays

blacksmith's *tea* loaf

Dried vine fruits are plumped up and infused with strong tea on top of the stove to make a moist and deliciously rich loaf. Serve thickly sliced, with or without butter, and a good cup of tea.

makes
1

V

Preheat the oven to 180°C (350°F) Gas 4.

Put the tea in a saucepan (non-aluminium) large enough to hold all the ingredients. Add the butter, fruit, spice, sugar, bicarbonate of soda and salt. Set over medium heat and bring to the boil, then reduce the heat and simmer gently for 5 minutes, stirring occasionally. Remove the pan from the heat and leave to cool for a couple of minutes.

Add the flour and baking powder to the pan and mix briefly, then stir in the eggs. When thoroughly mixed, scrape the mixture into the prepared tin and smooth the surface. Bake in the preheated oven for about 40 minutes, or until firm to the touch and a skewer inserted into the centre comes out clean. If the skewer comes out sticky, then bake for another 5 minutes and test again. Leave to cool, then turn out and remove the paper. The flavour is even better if the loaf is wrapped in foil and left overnight before cutting. Best eaten within 4 days. Can be frozen for up to 1 month.

300 ml strong black tea

115 g unsalted butter

350 g mixed dried fruit

2 teaspoons mixed spice

100 g light muscovado sugar

1 teaspoon bicarbonate of soda

¼ teaspoon sea salt

225 g spelt flour or plain wholemeal flour

1 teaspoon baking powder

2 large eggs, beaten

a 450-g loaf tin, greased and base-lined with greaseproof paper

pear & cranberry tartlets

serves 4

375 g ready-rolled puff pastry, defrosted if frozen

2 large ripe pears, peeled, halved and cored

25 g dried cranberries

25 g unsalted butter, chilled and diced

milk, for glazing

3 tablespoons granulated sugar

1 teaspoon cinnamon

pouring cream or crème fraîche, to serve

Having a packet of ready-rolled puff pastry in the fridge or freezer is always a great standby for an instant fruit tart. You can use practically any fruit; peaches, nectarines, apricots, plums, apples, blueberries, pineapple or a mixture of berries. Cinnamon will go with most fruits, or you could try seasoning plums with mace or apricots with nutmeg. Flaked almonds, walnuts and pecan nuts would also be good added to the fruits.

Preheat the oven to 220°C (425°F) Gas 7 and put in a non-stick baking tray to heat up.

Lightly flour a work surface and unroll the pastry. Use a sharp knife or a pizza wheel to cut it into 4 squares. Place a pear half in the centre of each pastry square and divide the dried cranberries between the squares. Scatter with the diced butter. Brush the edges with a little milk. Mix the granulated sugar with the cinnamon and sprinkle over the top.

Carefully slide the tarts onto the hot baking tray and return to the preheated oven to cook for about 35–40 minutes, or until the pastry is golden brown and crisp and the pears are tender. Serve whilst still warm with pouring cream or crème fraîche.

syrup banana rice cake

serves 8

75 g brown sugar

25 g unsalted butter

6 bananas, sliced

175 g white rice, cooked, drained and cooled

2 eggs, beaten

½ teaspoon vanilla extract

½ teaspoon grated nutmeg

50 g unrefined caster sugar

100 g self-raising flour

If South-east Asia were to have a version of tarte Tatin, this would be it – if you like sticky hot bananas and rice pudding, this was invented for you. It's also a surprising way to use up some leftover cooked white rice!

Preheat the oven to 180°C (350°F) Gas 4.

Put the brown sugar and butter in an ovenproof frying pan and set over medium-high heat. When melted and bubbling, add the bananas, in layers. Put the cooked rice, eggs, vanilla and nutmeg into a bowl and mix. Add the caster sugar and flour and stir until smooth. Spoon the mixture over the bananas, spreading it evenly with the back of a spoon. Transfer the pan to the preheated oven and bake for 35 minutes, or until set and golden. Leave to cool for 5 minutes, then turn out, banana side up, onto a large plate. Serve warm, at room temperature or cold.

chocolate soufflés

chocolate soufflés

These elegant soufflés belie the basic ingredients needed to make them. They are exceedingly light and meltingly soft.

serves **4**

V

180 g dark chocolate, chopped

150 ml double cream

3 large eggs, separated

2 tablespoons Cognac or brandy

2 large egg whites

3 tablespoons caster sugar

icing sugar, for sprinkling

4 soufflé dishes, 300 ml each, or 4 large coffee cups, greased and dusted with caster sugar

Stand the prepared soufflé dishes on a baking tray or in a roasting tin.

Put the chocolate into a heavy-based saucepan, pour in the cream, then set over very low heat and stir frequently until melted. Remove from the heat and stir in the egg yolks, one at a time, followed by the Cognac.

Preheat the oven to 220°C (425°F) Gas 7.

Put the 5 egg whites into a spotlessly clean, grease-free bowl and, using an electric whisk or mixer, whisk until stiff peaks form. Gradually whisk in the caster sugar to give a glossy, stiff meringue. The chocolate mixture should feel comfortably warm to your finger, so gently reheat if necessary. Using a large metal spoon, add a little of the meringue to the chocolate mixture and mix thoroughly. Pour the chocolate mixture on top of the remaining meringue and gently fold both mixtures together until just blended.

Spoon the mixture into the prepared soufflé dishes – the mixture should come to just below the rim. Bake in the preheated oven for 8–10 minutes, or until barely set – the centres should be soft and wobble when gently shaken. Sprinkle with icing sugar and eat immediately.

chocolate & rosemary pots

Chocolate and rosemary may sound an unusual combination but in fact the flavours go very well together. Remove the mousses from the refrigerator about 1 hour before serving so that they can return to room temperature.

serves **6**

V

300 ml single cream

2 sprigs of fresh rosemary, bruised

200 g dark chocolate, chopped

2 egg yolks

25 g unsalted butter

6 espresso cups or small ramekins

Put the cream and rosemary sprigs into a saucepan and heat slowly just to boiling point. Remove from the heat and leave to infuse for 20 minutes.

Strain into a clean pan, add the chocolate and heat very gently until the chocolate melts (don't let the mixture boil). Remove from the heat, leave to cool slightly, then stir in the egg yolks one at a time. Finally, add the butter, stirring until melted. Pour the mixture into the espresso cups and leave to cool. Chill for 2 hours but return to room temperature before serving.

zabaglione

2 large egg yolks

2 tablespoons sweet Marsala wine

2 tablespoons caster sugar

savoiardi or sponge fingers, for dipping

serves 2

Q

V

There is nothing quite as sensual as warm zabaglione served straight from the pan. The secret is not to let the mixture get too hot, but still hot enough to cook and thicken the egg yolks. The proportions are easy to remember: one egg yolk to one tablespoon sugar to one tablespoon Marsala, serves one person. It must be made at the last moment, but it doesn't take long and is well worth the effort.

Put the egg yolks, Marsala and sugar in a medium heatproof bowl (preferably copper or stainless steel) and beat with an electric whisk or a balloon whisk until well blended.

Set the bowl over a saucepan of gently simmering water but do not let the bowl touch the water. Do not let the water boil. Whisk the mixture until it is glossy, pale, light and fluffy and holds a trail when dropped from the whisk. This should take about 5 minutes. Serve immediately in warmed cocktail glasses with sponge fingers for dipping.

Note: To use up the egg whites left over after making this recipe, see recipes on pages 211, 227 and 233.

coffee crèmes brûlées

500 g single cream

5 teaspoons instant coffee granules

8 tablespoons sugar

4 egg yolks

2 tablespoons plain flour

1 tablespoon brandy

4 small ramekins

serves 4

V

Cracking through the glossy, burnt sugar crust and digging into the smooth, creamy, coffee custard below is sheer heaven.

Put the cream, coffee granules and half the sugar in a pan and warm gently until the coffee and sugar have dissolved, then remove from the heat.

Put the egg yolks in a bowl and beat in the flour to make a smooth paste. Gradually beat in the warm coffee cream mixture until smooth, then return to the pan. Heat very gently, stirring, for 5–10 minutes until you get a thick custard. Stir in the brandy, then pour the custard into the ramekins. Leave to cool, then cover and chill for at least 2 hours or overnight.

When you are ready to serve the crèmes brûlées, preheat the grill to high. Sprinkle each one with 1 tablespoon of the remaining sugar and grill for about 5 minutes until the sugar caramelizes. Remove from the heat, chill for a minute or two to set the brûlée, then serve.

zabaglione

index

recipe credits

Fiona Beckett
Fennel, leek & cauliflower soup
Piña colada sherbet

Susannah Blake
Coffee crèmes brûlées
Sticky fried bananas on toast

Tamsin Burnett-Hall
Chickpea, lemon & mint soup
Goulash meatballs with pasta
Smoked mackerel & bulgur
wheat salad

Maxine Clark
Blackberry cobbler
Brown sugar meringues
Buttered apricot betty
Carrots & courgettes with mint
Chicken liver risotto
Cranberry & orange streusel
crisp
Creamy tomato & bread soup
Gnocchi with herbs & semolina
Green herb risotto with white
wine & lemon
La ribollita
Mulled winter fruit crumble
Olive oil & garlic bruschetta
Pasta & bean soup
Plum crumble
Pot roast leg of lamb with
rosemary & onion gravy
Pumpkin & pea risotto
Ratatouille
'Roof tiles'
Sardines baked with garlic,
lemon, olive oil &
breadcrumbs
Slow-roasted tomatoes
Smoked mussel & leek risotto
Tomato & garlic bruschetta
Tomatoey green beans with
onion & fennel seeds
Zabaglione

Linda Collister
Blacksmith's tea loaf
Chocolate soufflés
Tuscan olive & rosemary bread

Ross Dobson
Baked brioche pudding
Baked courgette & tomato
risotto
Baked lemon pudding
Beef pie
Blackberry crumble
Carrot & lentil soup
Chilli & garlic steamed
mushrooms with polenta
Coq au leftover red wine
Egg, bacon & spinach pie
Lamb kefta tagine
Lemony chicken with spring
onions & pine nut couscous
Lemony mushrooms on toast

Lime pickle & veg biryani
Mushroom, spinach & potato
bake
Naked spinach & ricotta ravioli
with sage cream
Sage pork chops with kale
colcannon
Sausages with winter rösti
Shepherd's pie
Slow-cooked spiced pork belly
Smoky sausage & bean
casserole
Spaghetti with chilli &
courgettes
Spicy pork curry with lemon
rice
Spicy red vegetable soup
Spicy tomato, black bean & feta
dip
Swiss chard & white bean soup
Swiss chard, feta & egg pie
Thai-style fish with tomato
relish
Warm pasta salad with tuna,
chilli & rocket
Winter vegetable gratin
Winter vegetable tagine

Liz Franklin
Buttery jam tarts

Tonia George
Beef braised in rooibos tea
Chicken avgolemono
Chicken, garlic & watercress
soup
Ginger & caramel oranges
Lentil, spinach & cumin soup
Pea, smoked ham & mint soup
Split pea & sausage soup

Nicola Graimes
Bubble & squeak patties
Thai salmon fish cakes

Jennifer Joyce
Chicken noodle soup
Spaghetti and meatballs

Caroline Marson
Iced summer berries with hot
white chocolate sauce
Moroccan-style roasted
vegetables
Pear & cranberry tartlets
Pepperoni, red pepper &
crouton frittata
Spicy halloumi & chickpeas

Annie Nichols
Golden potato scones
Pizza with potatoes
Potatoes en papillote

Jane Noraika
Butternut squash & goats'
cheese gratin

Couscous tabbouleh
Green beans in tomato sauce
Polish cheesecake with berries
Rhubarb, ginger & banana
crumble
Roasted vegetable dauphinois

Elsa Petersen-Schepelern
Beef stock
Chicken stock
Dried pea & spelt soup
Fish stock
French onion soup
Mixed bean soup
Swedish yellow pea soup
Tomato soup
Tuna & bean salad
Tuscan tomato & bread salad
Vegetable stock

Louise Pickford
Bagna cauda
Banana fritters
Bread sauce
Carrot, orange & cumin dip
Chilli cornbread
Chocolate & rosemary pots
Frazzled eggs & smoked
gammon
Pesto
Rhubarb compote with yoghurt
Soda bread
Strawberries with black pepper
Tahini, yoghurt & garlic sauce
Tapenade

Rena Salaman
Falafel
Fried meatballs
Hoummus
Traditional Greek cheese pie

Jennie Shapter
Chickpea tortilla
Classic Spanish tortilla
Sausage, potato & onion tortilla
Spaghetti & rocket frittata
Sun-dried tomato frittata

Anne Sheasby
Thrifty tips

Fiona Smith
Chopped liver with zhoug
Greek barley salad
Sautéed greens
Tuna & caramelized onion pâté

Sonia Stevenson
Braised lamb shanks with
orange
Chicken & sweet potatoes
Choucroute garnie
Irish carbonnade
Oxtail in red wine
Red-cooked pork
Tuscan pork & bean casserole
Yankee pot roast

Linda Tubby
Fresh fried trout

Iced lemon crush
Spanish Migas with bacon

Sunil Vijayakar
Kofta curry

Fran Warde
Baked ham with layered
potatoes
Beef & carrot casserole with
cheesy dumplings
Blackberry & apple pie
Chicken in a pot
Chilli con carne
Curried lentils & spinach
Easy tuna fish cakes
Field mushroom tortilla
Golden butternut squash soup
Honeyed chicken wings
Lancashire hotpot
Mushroom risotto
Norwegian apple bake
Risotto primavera
Roast pork with baked apples
Spaghetti Bolognese
Steamed syrup pudding
Stuffed peppers
Syrup banana rice cake

Laura Washburn
Basic croissant pudding
Berry gratin
Braised beef brisket with carrots
Braised celery
Braised pork chops with
tomatoes
Cabbage soup
Cauliflower with anchovies
Chicken with tomatoes & olives
Cider pork with potatoes &
apples
Crêpes
Flourless chocolate cake
Lemon-spiced chicken
Orzo pilaf
Pumpkin & rice gratin
Roast chicken with bay leaves
Spareribs with orange glaze
Stuffed tomatoes

Lindy Wildsmith
Pot-luck summer pasta
Puttanesca pasta sauce
Quick Neapolitan tomato sauce

Toasted oat yoghurt & red
berries

photography credits

Key: a=above, b=below, r=right, l=left, c=centre.

Caroline Arber
Pages 75, 92, 99, 107, 150, 186

Martin Brigdale
Pages 3r, 9b, 10, 11bl, 28, 71, 79,
80, 83a, 104, 118, 126, 131,132,
135, 147, 157l, 161, 166, 182,
197a&c, 202, 206, 232, 235

Peter Cassidy
Pages 2, 5, 9c, 11al, 21, 23 both,
31, 34, 35b, 36, 42, 45, 49, 51c,
63, 64, 67, 72, 82, 97l, 178, 194,
210, 213, 214, 216, 221, 228

Nicki Dowey
Pages 1, 122

Gus Filgate
Pages 13c, 33 both

Tara Fisher
Pages 6, 97r, 100

Richard Jung
Pages 3c, 11ar, 35a&c, 40, 46,
51a, 68, 74 both, 83c&b, 84,
88, 103, 116, 117a&b, 121, 136,
143, 144, 148, 154, 177, 181,
196, 222, 227l

William Lingwood
Pages 13a, 14, 27, 162, 165, 169,
173, 190, 205

Diana Miller
Pages 3l, 13b, 18, 24

Noel Murphy
Pages 114, 189, 227r

David Munns
Pages 87, 140, 158, 201, 225, 231

William Reavell
Pages 12, 17, 197b, 199l

Yuki Sugiura
Pages 9a, 50, 51b, 56, 59, 60, 76

Debi Treloar
Pages 8, 139, 157r, 199r, 209, 218

Ian Wallace
Pages 11br, 43, 52, 55, 91, 125

Kate Whitaker
Pages 39, 95, 108, 111, 112, 113,
117c, 129 both, 149 all, 153,
170, 174, 185, 193